Volume 6, Issue 4 December 2002

Edited by Dr. Valerie Steele

Fashion Theory

The Journal of Dress, Body & Culture

Fashion Theory: The Journal of Dress, Body & Culture

Editor
Dr. Valerie Steele
The Museum at the Fashion Institute of Technology, E201
Seventh Avenue at 27th Street
New York, NY 10001-5992
USA
Fax: +1 212 924 3958
e-mail: valerie@fashiontheory.com

Book Reviews Editor
Christopher Breward
The London College of Fashion
20 John Princes Street
London W1M 0BJ

Exhibitions Reviews Editor
Alexandra Palmer
Royal Ontario Museum
100 Queen's Park, Toronto
Ontario M5S 2C6, Canada
Fax: +1 416 586 5877
e-mail: alexp@rom.on.ca

Please send all books for review to the Book Reviews Editor

Aims and Scope
The importance of studying the body as a site for the deployment of discourses is well-established in a number of disciplines. By contrast, the study of fashion has, until recently, suffered from a lack of critical analysis. Increasingly, however, scholars have recognized the cultural significance of self-fashioning, including not only clothing but also such body alterations as tattooing and piercing. *Fashion Theory* takes as its starting point a definition of 'fashion' as the cultural construction of the embodied identity. It aims to provide an interdisciplinary forum for the rigorous analysis of cultural phenomena ranging from footbinding to fashion advertising.

Anyone wishing to submit an article, interview, or a book, film or exhibition review for possible publication in this journal should contact Valerie Steele (at the address listed to the left) or the Editorial Department at Berg (150 Cowley Road, Oxford, OX4 1JJ, UK; e-mail: enquiry@bergpublishers.com).

Notes for Contributors can be found at the back of the journal.

ISSN: 1362-704X
www.fashiontheory.com

Ordering Information	Four issues per volume.	One volume per annum.	2002: Volume 6
By mail:	Berg Publishers, 150 Cowley Road, Oxford, OX4 1JJ, UK.		
By fax:	+44 (0) 1865 791165		
By telephone:	+44 (0) 1865 245104		
By e-mail:	enquiry@bergpublishers.com		
Inquiries	Editorial: Kathryn Earle, Managing Editor, e-mail: kearle@berg1.demon.co.uk		
	Production: Ian Critchley, e-mail: icritchley@bergpublishers.com		
	Advertising + subscriptions: enquiry@bergpublishers.com		
Subscription Rates:	Institutional base list subscription price: £89.00, US$145.00.	Individuals' subscription price: £35.00, US$55.00.	
Reprints of Individual Articles	Copies of individual articles may be obtained from the Publishers at the appropriate fees. Write to: Berg, 150 Cowley Road, Oxford, OX4 1JJ, UK.	Printed in the United Kingdom. DECEMBER 2002	

Indexed by the International Bibliography of Social Sciences; The MLA International Bibliography; ARTbibliographies, Clothing and Textile Arts Index and the Anthropological Index Online (AIO), the Royal Anthropological Institute of Great Britain and Ireland.

Page 359

Page 369

Page 387

Page 421

Page 441

Contents

Editor
Dr. Valerie Steele
The Museum at the Fashion
  Institute of Technology, E201
Seventh Avenue at 27th Street
New York, NY 10001-5992
USA

Fax +1 212 924 3958
e-mail: valerie@fashiontheory.com

Fashion Theory, Volume 6, Issue 4, pp. 357–358
Reprints available directly from the Publishers.
Photocopying permitted by licence only.

Letter from the Editor

I am pleased to report that the exhibition London Fashion, which was on display last year at The Museum at the Fashion Institute of Technology, was the recipient of the first Richard Martin Award for Museum Exhibitions by the Costume Society of America. Several of the designers prominently featured in London Fashion—Alexander McQueen, Hussein Chalayan, and Vivienne Westwood—also starred in Radical Fashion at the Victoria and Albert Museum. I was very interested in seeing how they were presented in Claire Wilcox's exhibition, especially since she had asked me to write the chapter on British designers for the V&A catalogue.

My first reaction was jealousy! I thought that Radical Fashion was a beautiful exhibition. The section devoted to Alexander McQueen, featuring his "Red Glass Slide and Ostrich Feather Dress," was especially breathtaking, as it drew on the theatrical presentation of his original fashion show of Spring/Summer 2001. Constructed from thousands of microscope slides hand-drilled and individually painted red, the dress brilliantly exemplified McQueen's often brutal explorations of the body. Also highly arresting was the V&A's section on Hussein Chalayan, which included an animated version of a video game in which models from his Ventriloquy collection shot at and smashed the shells of each other's dresses. As Bradley Quinn points out in his review of Radical Fashion,

"Chalayan's film presentation heralded a move away from static dress forms and live models, providing a platform to showcase experimental designs . . . cinematically that a designer may not be able to explore in a live show." I found the section on Vivienne Westwood disappointing, however, since it ignored her truly radical and influential punk, fetish, and new romantic fashions of the 1970s and 1980s. This absence was undoubtedly due to Claire Wilcox's emphasis on recent fashions of the 1990s through 2001, but it was unfortunate nevertheless.

Bradley Quinn questions whether Radical Fashion was truly "radical." It is certainly valid to ask, as he does, why certain clothes were included rather than others. "Gaultier, who brought the raw sex appeal of his conical bustiers and fetishistic corsetry to the Paris catwalk while making shocking attempts to transform the skirt into a menswear item, was represented in evening-gown silhouettes and unassuming garments," he writes, adding: "Curiously, the impact of sexually explicit garments on the notion of the radical was not addressed in the exhibition." He also asks why certain designers, such as John Galliano and Thierry Mugler were not included.

Without presuming to answer for Claire Wilcox, I can say, as a curator, that it is not always possible to include the clothes one most desires. Designers may no longer own certain ensembles, or they may insist on sending others of their own choosing. Sometimes they can not take part in one exhibition, because they have already promised to loan key objects to another museum.

For example, I know that Claire Wilcox is now in the process of organizing a major exhibition at the V&A on Versace. I know this, because I called Versace's New York office to try to borrow the Elizabeth Hurley safety-pin dress for an exhibition that I am organizing called Fashion, Italian Style. Since my show opens only a few weeks after her show ends, that particular dress may not be available. There will, however, be more than one hundred other clothing ensembles on display (including Versace), so please come see Fashion, Italian Style if you are in New York City any time between February 11 and April 12, 2003. Meanwhile, I would like to invite you to enjoy this issue of Fashion Theory, which includes another essay by Bradley Quinn on Hussein Chalayan—whose clothes, incidentally, have been practically fought over by museum curators around the world.

Yours sincerely,

Valerie F. Steele

Fashion Theory, Volume 6, Issue 4, pp. 359–368
Reprints available directly from the Publishers.
Photocopying permitted by licence only.
© 2002 Berg. Printed in the United Kingdom.

A Note: Hussein Chalayan, Fashion and Technology

Bradley Quinn

Bradley Quinn is a writer and curator who has worked as a fashion journalist and editor for publications and broadcasters on both sides of the Atlantic. He is the author of *Chinese Style* and his book *Techno Fashion* will be released by Berg Publishers in January 2003.

Hussein Chalayan is one of the most innovative fashion designers of our age. He draws heavily upon technology to revolutionize the form and function of clothing, often taking inspiration from the built environment and the body's relationship to it. Chalayan's clothes are minimal in look but maximal in thought; his fascination with architecture, aerodynamics, bodily form, and identity lead to designs based on concepts, or render his own interpretation of spatial dynamics. Chalayan's sense of the visual is ultimately true to his grasp of the practical and cultural needs resolved by clothing.

Chalayan rose to fashion fame soon after he received his B.A. degree from Central Saint Martin's School of Art in 1993. His final year collection, *The Tangent Flows*, is the now infamous series of buried garments that had been exhumed just before the show and presented with an accompanying text that explained the process. The ritual of burial and resurrection gave the garments a dimension that referenced life, death, and urban decay, in a process that transported garments from the world of fashion to the world of nature. The work attracted the attention of the London boutique Brown's, who borrowed the collection to feature in their window display. Since then, he has collaborated with architects, artists, textile engineers and set designers, won awards, and produced collections for other established fashion labels.

What makes Chalayan's work so intriguing is his ability to explore principles that are visual and intellectual, tracing the fabric of urban structures and interiors through tangibles like clothing, architecture, aeroplanes, and furniture; and through abstractions such as beauty, philosophy, and feeling. Chalayan's work represents a congruity of ideas that indicate fashion and architecture are coming closer together than ever before—far beyond the fashions of the 1920s that echoed the architectural lines of buildings. Chalayan's strategy is to integrate clothing with its surroundings, not by merely making dresses look architectural, but by rendering a comprehensive understanding of different environments and the diverse factors that create them. He reconciles the practical reasons for clothing while interpreting them as components of a modular environmental system where garments relate to larger architectural principles. Chalayan says, "One thing to keep in mind is that when fashion looks modular and structured, people automatically call it architectural when it isn't—it takes a lot of structuring to make a dress truly architectural. Architecture can be designed in a fluid and unstructured way that doesn't look architectural, but it is still architecture. I mean, you don't call buildings fashion just because they don't look architectural, so why call fashion architectural unless it really is?"

Chalayan sees all objects, structures, and architecture as externalizations of the body. His *Geotrophics* collection (Spring/Summer 1999) featured Chair Dresses that represented the idea of a nomadic existence and a completely transportable environment. This concept was later expanded in Chalayan's ground-breaking *After Words* (Fall/Winter 2000) collection. Presented at Sadler's Wells theatre in London, the show featured a bare, white stage flanked by asymmetrical planes on three sides and contained 1950s-style furniture that the models adapted as clothing in the show's finale and either carried or wore off the stage. The show was based on the idea of having to evacuate home during a time of war, hiding possessions when a raid was impending, and using the agency of clothing as the means to carry away possessions more quickly. The theme was painfully close to real life; it was an autobiographical expression of Chalayan's Turkish Cypriot roots and the political events that affected his childhood. The show's finale recalled the 1974 Turkish military intervention that divided Cyprus in half and displaced both Turkish and Greek Cypriots from their homes.

After Words expressed a political reality that articulated relationships between garments and cultural narratives, but was not intended to transform the garments into inhabited environments. *After Words* explored notions about expatriation and the idea of being able to transport an environment from one place to another in times of crisis. The Table Skirt and the entire set from the show were later featured in the Tate Modern's *Century City* exhibition in 2001, chosen because of their expression of the evolving dynamic between the built environment and the physical transience of urban life.

Some of the garments in the collection were equipped with pockets and compartments that would hold essential belongings, or fuse with other items of clothing so that they could be put on more quickly. "A part of the idea was camouflage, so that things could be left in an obvious place and still be there when people came home again. That was part of the concept behind the dresses, that they were something valuable disguised as chair covers that no one would take," Chalayan explained. "Things like that happened to my family in Cyprus. I heard stories about things that happened to them and everyone else. Somehow people would sneak back to their homes to get things that belonged to them—which they weren't allowed to do—so I was also showing how a space could be emptied little by little, almost in secret."

The space occupied by clothing is central to Chalayan's vision: clothing defines the intimate zone around the body, architecture a much larger one. In *After Words*, Chalayan expressed how either could become a danger zone and a refuge, a means of transportation for what could be carried and a camouflage for things left behind. Symbolically, the models were able to transport items from a "threatening" environment to a safe place, reestablishing the safety and familiarity associated with them in different surroundings. It is significant that they transported the garments by bringing them into contact with the body, rescuing them as one would carry a child to safety. Again, this referenced Chalayan's family experience. "All those things happened when I was a kid, but nobody forgets it," he said. "I was moved during the show. Of course my family was there watching the show, but at first they didn't realize what was going on. When they did, they were moved too."

Despite his education and long-term residency in London, Chalayan is true to his identity as a Turkish Cypriot, only recently coming to terms with being labeled as a British designer. "I'm grateful that I have a bi-cultural background," he said. "I was exposed to more things. You have more to respond to and you question things more." The idea of "national" style is problematic for the fashion world, where designers of diverse nationalities show in the fashion capitals. Chalayan seems to have more in common with Issey Miyake and Rei Kawakubo who show in Paris than any British designer showing in London. Fellow Turks Rifat Ozbek and Nicole Farhi are also acclaimed for their collections, but these bear no similarity to Chalayan's work at all. "Now I would say that I see myself as a British designer, because I was educated here and have had opportunities that I couldn't have in Cyprus. So in terms of discipline, yes, I am anglicized, but as for my sensibilities, my approach looks at architecture, environments and technology which means I am not like most other designers here," he said.

Chalayan never harbored a deep-rooted desire to become a fashion designer. As a child, he wanted to be a pilot, and then considered training to be an architect. Both professions have influenced his career as a designer: the former in the flight-path prints he began exploring in Fall 1995, his "Aeroplane" dresses and his "Kite" dresses; the latter evident in the spatial awareness directing the relationship between his garments and the body, and his use of architectural proportions to amplify their interplay with their surroundings. "To me there are two sides to fashion's engagement with the built environment. One is the lifestyle concept that magazines like *Wallpaper** are pushing, showing what you should wear, how you should live, what furniture, which flat—selling the lifestyle as a fashionable status thing," Chalayan said. The commercial relationship between interior design and fashion promotes a lifestyle dimension, where mainstream designers are selling household products alongside clothing, offering consumers an overall "look." "The other, and the one where I come from, is that everything around us either relates to the body or to the environment. I think of modular systems where clothes are like small parts of an interior, the interiors are part of architecture, which is then a part of an urban environment. I think of fluid space where they are all a part of each other, just in different scales and proportions," he said.

The series of architectural dresses Chalayan designed for the *before minus now* collection (Spring/Summer 2000) evolved through his collaboration with b consultants, a London-based firm of architectural engineers, with whom he continued to explore his affinity with architecture. The dresses featured wire-frame architectural prints against static white backgrounds, generated by a computer program that allows designers to draw within a range of three-dimensional perspectives inside an architectural landscape. The images were then transferred onto silk and cotton fabrics using a mechanized fabric-printing process. "I have always been interested in technology, and there are elements of technology in my clothes. And I work in a cross-disciplinary way with people in other fields who contribute to what I am doing. I am interested in forms generally, not just in clothing but in other things too." In the *Echoform* collection (Fall/Winter 1999) Chalayan created thought-provoking designs like leather dresses inspired by car interiors to represent "externalizing speed and putting it back on the body"—and mimicked aeroplane interiors by attaching padded headrests to dresses to evoke thoughts on speed, spatiality and well-being.

The *before minus now* collection also featured the "Remote Control" dress which amplified Chalayan's interest in technology, and proved to be a ground-breaking triumph. The dress was based on the Aeroplane dresses series made by means of the composite technology used to construct aircraft, and incorporated the aerodynamics of aeroplane travel into its form and aesthetic. The contours of the dresses are characteristic of vehicle construction, while their hard exterior gives them shield-like properties reminiscent of snails and crustaceans. Gaston Bachelard would have regarded such objects as "inhabited shells" that "invite daydreams of refuge." (Bachelard 1994: 107) But in Chalayan's case, it is the formation rather than the form itself that inspired him to fabricate a technologized environment directly onto the surface of the body.

Chalayan's fashion shows often suggest fine art or performance more than fashion, which Chalayan regards as coincidental. "I am not really up to date with what is going on in the art world or the performance world," he explained. "I just do what is good for my work. As a designer I have lots of ideas about how clothes should be worn and creating an atmosphere around them. A lot of these ideas remain invisible until I have a show, and then I can put them across in the show." His fashion shows are characterized by minimal sets and a mood of suspense, incorporating elements of contemporary interiors, urban architecture, and geometric structures. Chalayan succeeds in taking the audience to a space governed by his concepts alone, which some critics liken to the kind of thrill assoc- iated with Diaghilev's productions early last century.

Panoramic (Fall/Winter 1998) was one of Chalayan's most dramatic fashion collections. The collection culminated in the idea of infinity, which was expressed in a surreal cityscape of geometric forms and distorted images. Chalayan created an environment that eradicated perimeters and built environments and blurred cultural boundaries, camouflaging the body by merging it into the surroundings or multiplying its image in mirrors placed at intersecting angles. The models were distorted into generic shapes and unified by architectural proportions; cones were fixed to the top of the head and faces and bodies swathed in black to obscure their identity. The purpose behind these dramatic silhouettes was to create a non-distinct cultural/ethnic identity. As Chalayan explored the idea of representing nature in the collection, he broke it down into its most basic graphic representation—pixels. Body and clothing were then merged into a digital landscape, which was recreated in enlarged cube-shaped pixels carried by a column of models clad in somber bodysuits as they processed slowly down the catwalk. The overall effect was that of experiencing spatial geometry created by bodies and cloth, interchanging the basis of fashion's relationship to the body and its surroundings.

Chalayan approaches the body as a site of exploration, investigating its physical and metaphorical relationship to the world around it. Chalayan's clothes are futuristic in their ability to use the body as a site for both formal expression and experimentation, transforming it into a vehicle for meditations on fashion, design, physicality and on the kind of intangibles that fashion rarely addresses. The conceptual and theoretical inspirations behind his garments are each played out across the body, often inverting traditional views of sexuality, eroticism, embodiment and proportions. "The body, in some respects, is the biggest symbol of tradition," Chalayan said. "That is why I am interested in re-animating certain thoughts around it, because you can alter the idea of the body in the way you present it."

Chalayan had been exploring the interaction between the body and technology for some time, expressing it on the catwalk in his *Panoramic* collection and several seasons later in his *Echoform* collection (Fall/Winter 2000). The Altitude project was based on exploring the relationship of the body's inherent mobility on the creation of forms that give it speed. "With Altitude I wanted to recreate environmental systems that mirror how the body moves. Thinking of speed led me to focus on car interiors which generated the idea of ergonomically amplifying the body's own speed and movement. I saw speed as something created by technological means to enhance the body's natural capacity to move quickly," Chalayan explained.

Figure 1
Erin O'Connor models the "Memory Wire Dress" for Chalayan's before minus now collection (spring/summer 2000). The dress is constructed with electric coils that expand, opening "like the flowers that remember how to take several forms." The dress is controlled by the wearer but operates independently of the body, a theme Chalayan continues to explore through technical innovation. Photograph by Chris Moore.

As Chalayan's work engages further with technological systems, he is pioneering garments that place wireless technology, electrical circuitry and automated commands directly onto the body's surface. His Remote Control dress (Spring/Summer 2000) was a hi-tech triumph that married fashion to technology and technology to the body, establishing a dialogue between the body and the environment. "The dress expressed the body's relationship to a lot of invisible and intangible things—gravity, weather, flight, radio waves, speed, etc.," Chalayan said. "Part of it is to make the invisible tangible, showing that the invisible can transform something and say something about the relationship of the object—the dress in this case—between the person wearing it and the environment around it."

The dress, like those in the Aeroplane series, was designed by means of the composite technology used by aircraft engineers, mirroring the systems that enable remote-control aeroplanes to fly. It is made from a combination of glass fiber and resin, molded into two smooth, glossy, pink-colored front and back panels that fasten together by metal clips. Each panel is encased within grooves two millimeters in width that run throughout the length of the dress. These seams create the only textural differences in the dress, revealing interior panels made in translucent white plastic, accentuated by lighting concealed within the solar plexus panel and the left side elevating panel. The dress is designed to remain on the ground, where the principles behind it also mirror the "intelligent" systems controlling and regulating the functions of modern buildings. This establishes a new affinity between the human and the environment, mediated by clothing designed to be intimately involved with their wearer's activities.

Starlab, the now-defunct research laboratory pioneering technologized clothing, developed prototype garments that could be programmed to anticipate and respond to the wearer's needs by communicating wirelessly with remote systems. Charmed Technology, a research organization exploring the potentials of wireless clothing, conducted similar studies with wireless technology to adapt it for fashion. Although their prototypes featured state-of-the-art technology that provided the wearer with a broad range of functions, they never evolved into a finished model before the projects were terminated in 2001. Chalayan's Remote Control Dress, though less sophisticated, was the first wireless device to be presented as a fully functioning fashion garment. The Remote Control Dress is a ground-breaking achievement on many levels, not least because it showed that the technological principles behind it could be achieved in fashion as well as science.

Chalayan described the dress' cyborgian attributes as "something of a side effect." The Remote Control Dress was not designed specifically to explore the relationship of technology to the body, but to examine how the form of the garment could evolve around the body in a spatial relationship to its environment. "If you alter the way the body comes across in the space around it, then the body alters everything in the space that affects it," Chalayan said. "The dress can also be transformed invisibly by the environment. The idea was a technological force between the environment and the person." Extending the function of a dress beyond clothing is central to Chalayan's work, and the Remote Control dress demonstrates that garments are capable of interaction with other humans and computerized systems distant in time and space.

The Remote Control Dress lines the body with computer devices and remote-control communication that aligns it to other systems. This reveals how technological enhancement means that the wearer must allow technology to come uncomfortably close to the body, all the while knowing that the systems themselves are ambivalent, capable of many contradictory uses. As the wearer puts on the Remote Control Dress, it literally becomes a cog in the machine. Through the technology in the dress, the body could then be linked to other machines, and linked to other bodies also linked to machines. This would connect the wearer to larger bodies of people, businesses, and governments through the agency of wireless communication technologies. This gives the axis of fashion and technology another dimension, signaling the integration of the constructor and the constructed.

The concept of the human cyborg resulted from Manfred Clynes and Nathan Kline's theories of how humans could survive in extraterrestrial environments by being equipped with medical implants and prostheses. (Clynes and Kline 1960: 26–7, 75–6) More recently, Donna Haraway has expanded this definition to suggest that cyborgs represent more than the classical distinction between nature and artifice, as "a hybrid of machine and organism, a creature of social reality as well as a creature of fiction." (Haraway 1999: 50–9) In Haraway's thinking, those surfing the net, designing virtual bodies or operating equipment can be considered cyborgs, since their own nervous systems operate in direct connection with the artificial intelligence of the machine.

The cyborg body is a paradox of technological power and control, mirroring how the fashioned body is also determined by the ideals and values of a wider society. As scientists define the categories of cyborg bodies, the attributes of the fashioned body can also be identified in their studies. According to the research of Chris Hables Gray, Steven Mentor and Heidi Figueroa-Sarriera, technologies of the body can enhance it in four categories: they can be *restorative*, replacing lost functions, lost limbs, and failed organs; *normalizing*, creating a generic aesthetic while imposing technologized bodies as social or esthetical norms; *reconfiguring*, like the performance artist Stelarc, who equips the body with additional limbs or communication systems; or merely *enhancing* by increasing vision, optimizing mobility, hearing, etc. (Hables Gray *et al.*). In fashion terms, the cyborg body is for the most part *reconfiguring* and *enhancing* through products like sunglasses, spectacles, mobile phones, palm pilots, and even athletic shoes.

In addition to containing the principles of the *reconfiguring* and *enhancing* categories, the Remote Control dress suggests *normalizing* properties as it charts the techno-sexualization of the body. In its ability to reveal/conceal erogenous zones and shape the body into a uniform feminine silhouette, the dress forecasts the future means of equipping and manipulating the body to conform to body ideals and dynamics of sex appeal. The structural architecture of the Remote Control Dress echoes the attributes of a fashioned body rather than an organic body. The structure of the dress forms an exoskeleton around the body, incorporating elements of body consciousness; its contours mimic the curves of the fashioned female body, arcing dramatically inward at the waist and outward in the hip region, echoing the silhouette of the corset and the crinoline. This gives the dress a defined hourglass shape that incorporates principles of corsetry in its design, emphasizing a conventionally feminine shape, while creating a solid structure that simultaneously masks undesirable body proportions.

As the dress's panels and components are activated to open and close, it evokes the allure of exposed skin and flesh, while concealing the body underneath its lining. "I made a tulle dress to be worn under the remote control dress, so that's what you see when it opens. I don't show erogenous zones in an obvious, clichéd way," he said. "Sexiness doesn't come from what you wear, or from your physical appearance—it's all to do with feeling good about yourself." The sensuality associated with revealing and concealing the body is central to Chalayan's work, which challenges the way fashion defines erogenous zones, and avoids creating clothes that scream sex appeal. Chalayan views these pleasure centers as highly individual; zones to be explored and identified on individual bodies rather than dictated by fashion. In 1997 he sent models onto the catwalk wearing black chadors of varying lengths and nothing else, alluding to fashion's continual shift of erogenous zones around the female body arises in response to changing ideals.

The dress confronts one of the most profound issues raised by new technologies: the possibility that human identities would take on the properties of machines or be at their mercy. Though the wearer can access external symptoms via the remote, inherent in the dress is a sinister reversal—the potential for those systems to control the wearer. The interface of flesh and technology is both thrilling and terrifying, if technology holds the potential to override the body's commands and take control of it before the wearer is able to escape.

As a technologized object the dress is loaded with symbolic value: it is a tool of communication, a man–machine hybrid, and a hallmark of scientific progress. For fashion, it achieves innovations never thought possible, and amplifies the potential fashion has always had to interact and communicate. As the dress interacts with its immediate environment, or performs maneuvers originating from a command center, it enables the body to extend its range of movements and control beyond arm's reach. The dress makes it clear that the fashioned mechanization of the body and the integration of both into a larger technological system produces a whole new range of practices, possibilities, and aesthetics that transgresses the body/machine boundary.

This marks a radical departure from a world where distinctions between body and machine, body and dress, present and distant, natural and artificial once seemed clear. This illustrates how, as Michel Foucault described, social and cultural discourses construct our bodies in a way that makes us as analogous to a machine as possible. The design of the dress is imbued with technologies that make interaction efficient, productive, and empowered, akin to the machine-like principles of controlled automation. The presence of hi-tech systems in fashion fuses its body conscious ideals with a belief in automation, speed and accuracy as the means to achieve it.

While, historically, fashion has defined the human body according to social values, technological progress is radically changing the way it is perceived. As Chalayan's work reflects these changes, his Remote Control Dress showed what science could not yet represent: the icon of the technological age. The Remote Control Dress reminds us that we are always embodied, while showing that the future choices of embodiment, like choices of clothing, may not always be simple. As Chalayan continues to expand his thinking behind these representations, his clothing requires a body with confidence to carry off clothing still heavy with the thought process that created it.

Chalayan is among the most ambitious innovators working with fashion today, those whose work avoids commercially minded values and fashion trends. In ignoring these restrictions, they have set up a critical discourse of the principles of clothing. His work imbues garments with architectural, environmental, and technological principles. As he explores fashion's relationship to the built environment, he reveals the extent to which fashion, interiors and architecture can be truly integrated in design. "This way of thinking about fashion is still quite new to the fashion world, but it's what is moving things forward. The fashion audience doesn't really know about technology or architecture," Chalayan explained, "but they soon will."

References

Bachelard, Gaston. 1994. *The Poetics of Space*. Boston, MA: The Beacon Press.

Gray, Chris Hables, Steven Mentor and Heidi Figueroa-Sarriera (eds). 1995. *The Cyborg Handbook*. London: Routledge.

Haraway, Donna. "A manifesto for cyborgs." In Gill Kirkup *et al.* (eds), *The Gendered Cyborg*. New York: Routledge.

Clynes, Manfred E. and Nathan S. Kline. 1960. "Cyborgs and Space." *Astronautics* September 1960: 26–7, 75–6.

Fashion Theory, Volume 6, Issue 4, pp. 369–386
Reprints available directly from the Publishers.
Photocopying permitted by licence only.

A Longing for Perfection: Neoclassic Fashion and Ballet

Judith Chazin-Bennahum

Judith Chazin-Bennahum is a Professor of Theater and Dance at the University of New Mexico and a former ballerina with the Metropolitan Opera Ballet Company when Antony Tudor was Artistic Director. She has also written *Dance in the Shadow of the Guillotine* and *The Ballets of Antony Tudor*.

The late eighteenth century's fascination with classical dress parallels its intriguing new discourse with the body and the classical body. Dressed in soft, slender drapery, women returned to an idealized, ritualized experience of democracy, of equality, of the recognition that clothing has transformative values. The revealed body becomes the means through which the evolving meanings of political and social life in Greece and Rome are reinvented as circumstances change.

(Porter 1999: 13).

A brief resurgence of interest in classical antiquity began before the French Revolution in the 1780s and ended after Napoleon's reign in 1815. This wasn't necessarily a new preoccupation with antiquity, which was established during the Renaissance and later found recognition especially in the stunning theater of Racine and Corneille during the era of Louis XIV. For comic relief at that time, Molière enjoyed parodying mythic characters in his comédie-ballets. Mythological themes had been *de rigueur* in opera, theater and ballet for centuries.

Radically different in the neoclassicism of the late eighteenth and early nineteenth centuries is its embodiment in clothing, in feminine fashions and in masculine and feminine costumes on stage. The men of the time did not have the courage to sport togas or tunics. A variety of sources are responsible for its importance to clothing and costume—discoveries in archeology, the shift to historical accuracy in costumes for mythological plots, Enlightenment attitudes toward clothing strongly influenced by English modes, a blending of Boulevard costume practices with the Opéra's, and pleasure in the revelation of the female body. Essentially neoclassicism was the movement that freed the body in a sartorial switch from heavy, glittering embroidery and amplified skirts to the white, columnar lines of the tunic.

Neoclassicism engendered a remarkable shift in the aesthetics of clothing, "The female body lost its extremely defined waist in the 1780s and

Figure 1
Costume Parisien, example of A la Paysanne, the new fashion. Courtesy Cabinet des Estampes.

gained a soft, long skirt line with indented material, typical of the chiton, to permit free movement of the legs" (Hollander 1993: 117). The female body took on a new personality, it was reborn! The look of the breasts became round and full or "two well-defined hemispheres," rather than the eighteenth-century pushed up and bumpy look.

Flowing, transparent tunics revealed and idealized the female body, and especially recognized that this creature not only had legs to stand on, but also had an exciting sexual attraction in the new attire. However, the dresses were more suited to the climate of Greece. Sometimes the muslin was dampened so that it clung to the body in imitation of the folds of the Greek dresses (Laver 1995: 152). The new fashion greatly enhanced the young girl's figure, which also accounted for its great popularity. "This was the first time in the history of fashion that there had been any such

Figure 2
Madame de Staël and her daughter Albertine. Portrait by Vigée Lebrun, Courtesy of the Coll. Château de Coppet.

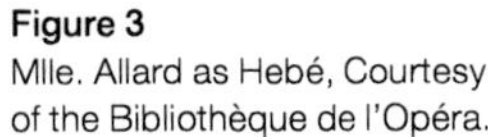

Figure 3
Mlle. Allard as Hebé, Courtesy
of the Bibliothèque de l'Opéra.

revival of a bygone mode. It was also the first time that a fashion had
been introduced which was especially attuned to the young" (Ewing 1971:
44). During this time, children's fashions, in that they were simple and
easy to wear, began to influence adult clothing (Boucher 1983: 303).

The new style replaced a highly formulaic and artificial dress form that
suited an arrogant aristocracy. Their living spaces were not designed for
relaxed, easy access to salons and daily meetings. On the contrary, room
proportions seem eminently small compared with our tastes today. The
eighteenth-century royal body deliberately forced itself into those spaces
with the court costume and all its accoutrements—paniers, lace, feathers,
jewels, large wigs, and high-heeled shoes with buckles. The steel corset
provided the framework for this architecture that pushed the breasts up

and emphasized a wasp waistline. Women's forms, their sensuality, adapted to the *règles de jeux* that permitted them to seek power where they could. Small, mincing steps gave the impression of the inflated royal bottom moving like a floating ship maneuvering itself through the wicked waters of the court. These exaggerated raiments were by no means worn by all levels of the population; however, they represented the power and the glory all looked to and respected. The aristocracy lived in a coveted, hermetic environment that paid little attention to the wider world. But travelers, artists, and intellectuals from all fields began to affect the culture of the time.

Archeological revelations and writings by Johann Joachim Winckelmann (1717–1768) threw light on Greek influences in Roman art and architecture. The 1738 discovery of art and artifacts in Italy's Pompeii and Herculaneum brought a new and lively awareness to the ancient world. In 1750, books of engravings and other pictures helped to publicize and popularize the draped gods of Pompeii and Herculaneum. Excavations of ancient amphora and Greek artifacts were unearthed and sent to the British Museum by Sir William Hamilton. He published his *Illustrations of Greek Vases* in 1770 and twenty years later married Emma Hamilton when he was ambassador to Naples.

Implicit in the neoclassic costume revival was the fact that Greek vases and sculpture, as well as Roman imitations, were not just archeology, or ethnographic proof of other cultures' artifacts, but forms of art with clear aesthetic and ideological intentions. Art informed the stage, as it should, and the audience liked it because the vision it held spoke the truth to them. The moving sculptures of the Elgin Marbles recalled a past where the principles of democracy were born and ideals of philosophy and behavior were pronounced. One particular book, *Travels of Anarcharsis* by the Abbé Barthélémy, encouraged many people to return to the past. It was a fourth-century BCE evocation of Philip of Macedonia's reign. The beauty of the Greek past helped to restore brotherhood and "invited people to identify with it" (Starobinski 1988: 166). Costumes for the stage and clothing on the street became "expressive" of the new French citizen, one who believed in freedom and the more personal self.

Even the queen needed to express herself. In the 1780s, under the influence of Marie Antoinette, Vigée-Lebrun's portraits, and English style or *à l'anglaise*, the chemise dress came into fashion. Yielding to English influences on local gossip and chatter, in 1783 Marie Antoinette rebelliously asked Vigée-Lebrun to paint a portrait of her in a "chemise" with her hair unpowdered and unwigged. The result of this portrait was the style *chemise à la reine*. Revolutionary in its simplicity, in its early form it was merely a tube of white muslin with a drawstring at the neck and a sash at the waist. One of the explanations for the origins of this dress was that the style was first borrowed from Creole women by the ladies of Bordeaux and was the forerunner of the muslin gowns worn during the next thirty years (Delpierre 1997: 109). The light color gave the shape

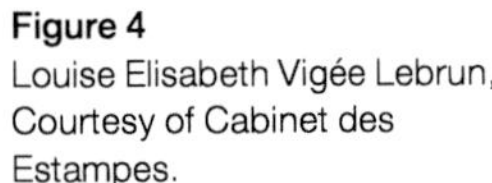

Figure 4
Louise Elisabeth Vigée Lebrun,
Courtesy of Cabinet des
Estampes.

and quality of draping a lovely aura. "Coming from the French West Indies (where indigo grew, giving the dresses a bright bluish-white hue), it was popularized by Marie Antoinette and from her court spread all over Europe" (Ribeiro 1983: 15). Vigée-Lebrun painted Marie-Antoinette twenty-five times.

Political relations between England and France became an important factor in this fashion. When wars led to the British Blockade, ports of entry that provided particular products such as silks or feathers were closed and fashions of the moment changed. The use of cotton was particularly suited to the tunic line of Greek statuary.[1] "Newly fashionable fabrics such as printed cotton and fine muslin were widely worn; when silk was worn it was often silk gauze, to provide the fluttering, floating look popular in the 1780s, or painted silk from the East" (Ribeiro 1983: 15).

Early on, England began to import cotton yarns via the East India Company when it was founded in 1612. It brought in costly fabrics such as calico from Calcutta and fine muslins from Mosul, Iraq. The East India's monopoly of trade with India ended in 1813 when the West Indies began to supply large quantities of raw cotton. They found further supplies in America, Mexico, and Peru. "By 1800 the cotton industry had overtaken the woolen one in Britain. As early as 1791, 38,000 black people were transported to the cotton plantations of America, which was more than half the total European slave trade for that year" (Ewing 1984: 63). Sad and devastating that slavery in South America, the West Indies and America increased as a result of fashion.

Discussion of this central moment in fashion history focuses on the newly-discovered female body. One reason for the popularity of the soft material and lines without corsets, was that breast-feeding was slowly

Figure 5
Costume Parisien, Demi-Négligé, Cabinet des Estampes.

gaining in popularity due to the works of Locke and Rousseau, with encouragement from leading women thinkers. Enlightenment writers disputed the contemporary need for uncomfortable opulence and ostentation as it reflected undemocratic notions. The Philosophes promoted a realignment of values in French social and political institutions and babies were included in this narrative. A mother could more comfortably nurse a baby with that kind of clothing. "Breastfeeding became fashionable! To call attention to this change in attitude about women's bodies, women also walked around with breasts showing" (Browne 1987: 52).

The fashion in the street dictated that a new shoe shape be worn with the tunic style of dress. Neoclassic fashions called for sandal-like small heels or heelless slippers tied about the ankles with satin ribbons. The ribbons secured the shoe on the foot and created the impression of a Greek sandal. This petite slipper began to grace the ballet studio as well. The discomfort of wearing a shoe smaller than one's natural size could be endured as the young girl was trained from an early age to bear pain.[2]

> The developing fashionable ideal had evolved a very narrow, light, flexible heelless slipper, constructed with a sole slightly too small for the wearer. The fabric of the upper, wrapping closely around the foot, compressed the bones together and encouraged them into a slender, elongated elegance demanded by the mode.
>
> (Squire 1974: 153)

Private gatherings were the site of dance improvizations in neoclassic garb. Mme Récamier, dear friend of Mme de Staël, often danced for others in her tunic and shawl. In the last two decades of the eighteenth century, the notorious Emma Hamilton (wife of Sir William and lover of Lord Nelson) created a performance art, improvizational *tableaux vivants* entitled "Attitudes." Inspired by her husband's revelatory book on Greek statues, she performed different pictorial moments while draped in soft materials, a living embodiment in these poses. She was termed Sir William's "Gallery of Statues," and described as being, "Fluid, graceful, sublime and heroic."[3] "In a marvelous way, according to her contemporaries, she could thus give new life to ancient figurations . . . one has to emphasize their broad resonance in the fashion and taste of society that neoclassical aestheticians believed, somewhat ingenuously, could be modified simply by appealing to the classical ideals of simplicity and purity" (Falcone 1996: 244).

At the Opéra any fashion became institutionalized so that the breath of fresh air that came with neoclassic attire rapidly installed itself as irreplaceable. "Rather quickly the antique style imposed new conventions that were as unrealistic as those that came before: the required flesh colored tights, the filmy tunic, the supple ballet slipper necessary to execute the pirouettes, which predicted the next design of the point shoe" (Christout 1965: 96).

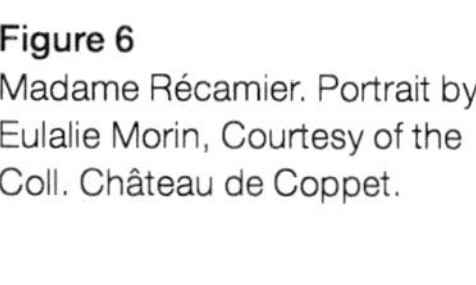

Figure 6
Madame Récamier. Portrait by
Eulalie Morin, Courtesy of the
Coll. Château de Coppet.

In the myth ballets, the short, light transparent tunic for dance became
common with the radical tendency to reveal the woman's body on stage.
This is confirmed by a review in the 26 November 1791, *Mercure de
France* of the opera *Diane et Endymion*, in which Mlle Saulnier "wore a
costume of almost transparent simplicity . . . She appeared almost naked,
yet her bearing banishes any licentious thought. She brings to mind those
beautiful Spartan women on the banks of the Eurotas, who, to borrow a
phrase from Rousseau, were clothed only in public respect" (Guest 1996:
331–2). In an earlier article on 20 November 1791, in the *Chronique de
Paris*, Victoire Saulnier is praised for her performance in the same opera:
"We must give her credit for being almost the only dancer at the Opéra
to have adopted an authentic costume." (Ibid.)

At the Archives Nationales, in cluttered boxes with folders of the Opéra's accounts and spending, a document lists the *tunique blanche* as the favored costume for dancers, probably the corps, from 1800 onward. Accessories were tights, flower or laurel crowns, tambours for Terpsichore, and so forth. This confirmed the shift to a more uniform, simplified profile for the *corps de ballet* and recognized that ballet technique could more easily be explored if the dancer were wearing less cumbersome attire.

The value of this filmy *tissu* was that the shortening of the dress and the use of transparent material in its construction led to the introduction of *maillot* or tights, a combination of long stockings with skin-tight knickers. The invention of this garment is generally attributed to Maillot— a costumier at the Opéra at the beginning of the nineteenth century who died in 1838.

The *Maître de Ballet* of the Opéra, Pierre Gardel, discovered during the Reign of Terror that he could keep his head and satisfy the early revolutionaries as well as audiences if he reverted to the popular mythological themes. Under the prophetic influence of Noverre and Angiolini, Gardel produced the romanticized myths as ballet-pantomimes with dancers who could act, and who gave their movements and gestures an expression of feelings that we associate with romantic literature. *Télémaque dans l'Isle de Calypso* and *Psyché* in 1790, and in 1793 *Le Jugement de Paris* succeeded beyond all expectations. Later during the Empire, it was natural for Gardel and other choreographers at the Opéra to appeal to Napoléon's conservative taste for antiquity. Each of Gardel's myth-based ballets became so popular that they still remain on the lists of the most well-attended performances at the Opéra. Certainly, their touching stories and the more emotive manner of presentation gave them tremendous impact. The transformations enhanced their visual splendor. Since Gardel's teacher was the distinguished choreographer Jean-Georges Noverre, he emphasized carefully structured scenarios and dancing with gestural power.

Télémaque dans l'isle de Calypso (23 February 1790) tells the story of Ulysses' son who returns to Calypso's island where he discovers true love. Télémaque's tunic and mantle displayed the gentle lines of a draped dress to the knee with decorated hem and neckline. Calypso's revealing skirt fell above the knee. A rope-like belt defined a high waistline over a sleeveless bodice that hung over the skirt as seen in pictures of Greek women. Sandals were the preferred shoe.

The ballet *Psyché* (14 December 1790) depicts the tale of the young goddess upstart who attempts to compete with Venus while falling madly in love with Cupid, Venus' son. Psyché endures classic suffering for her sins while the stage is filled with dazzling scenic spectacles. What contributed to the fortune of this ballet was her costume. The *robe à la Psyché* became one of the most touted fashions of the time. *Le Journal de la Mode et du Goût* of 25 December 1790 mentioned that this costume was tastefully designed to suggest one breast was exposed. The dressmaker

Figure 7
Mlle. Clotilde as Calypso,
Courtesy of the Bibliothèque
de l'Opéra.

Mme Teillard offered the *robe à la Psyché* for sale at her shop (Guest 1996: 325). However it is doubtful that women actually wore one breast exposed on stage; sources of the time do not confirm this practice. For a brief period after Napoleon, dancers wore as little as possible, although there is no mention that their breasts actually were nude. A few society women did indeed expose one breast in social situations. It was a sensational as well as suggestive gesture.

In *Le Jugement de Paris* (6 March 1793), gods and shepherds dance together while Paris takes his time falling in love with Oenone. First, Paris must judge "the most beautiful," a contest between Venus, Minerva, and Juno, and of course decides that Venus merits the title of most beautiful woman in the world. Ultimately, he chooses the lovely young Oenone for himself. In *Le Jugement de Paris*, historical accuracy gave way to

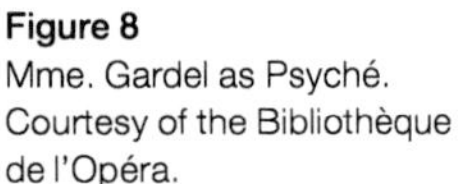

Figure 8
Mme. Gardel as Psyché.
Courtesy of the Bibliothèque
de l'Opéra.

convenience as the dancers no longer wore the traditional Greek coth-
urnes, but lightly sported the modified Phrygian sandal in which one
moved much more easily (Christout 1965: 205).

Jacques-Louis David institutionalized the cult of the antique during
the Jacobin period when the guillotine also known as "La Veuve" was
effectively wiping out the aristocracy and clergy. David designed the
Revolutionary Festivals that attracted the Parisians and French people
to the streets to celebrate their goddesses of reason and Liberty. The floats
were decorated with symbols and artifacts that brought ancient Greece
back to life. The dancing girls who graced these moving panoplies wore
white tunics with beautiful drapery.

Figure 9
Robe à la Psyché, Courtesy of
the Cabinet des Estampes.

At the Opéra, it is believed that the artist/costumer, Jean-Simon Berthélémy initiated the antique style at the ballet when Pierre Gardel was
dancing master. Berthélémy was brought in as costumier in 1787 at the
Paris Opéra by Ménagéot, who was originally appointed to the position
but took a more prestigious job and gave his to Berthélémy. Berthélémy
succeeded Boquet as "dessinateur en titre des costumes de l'Opéra" and
remained until 1807 when Ménagéot recovered his original position
(Sandoz 1979). Boquet's tenure lasted through the middle years of the
eighteenth century. He was a decorative artist, greatly skilled in creating
delicate Rococo confections that were firmly based on the stiff and stand-
ardized costume shape and seemed to be out of touch with trends in the
artistic community. His sketches of exotic people, Indians, classical gods,
furies, appear sprightly, delicate, and as formal as Bérain's a century earlier.

Figure 10
Costume illustration by Jean-Simon Berthélémy of *Proserpine*. Courtesy of the Bibliothèque de l'Opéra.

But following him, a serious change was afoot. Unlike many of the Opéra's scene and costume designers, both Berthélémy and Ménagéot were academic painters who had studied in Rome and learned the standard rules of painting techniques that brought neoclassicism and draperies onto the opera stage. Berthélémy's talents as a ceiling painter and designer of historical pictures demonstrated that he understood beautifully the value of a dramatic setting. His designs depicted the perfect moment to display his costumes, showing the characters during an expressively vivid scene. Another important contribution was his insistence that there were rules to protect the design of the costumes and scenery, a kind of early copyright. He also wished that the costumes be properly maintained and cataloged by the Chief Tailor. No doubt, one of the reasons for the great success of Gardel's myth-based ballets during revolutionary times was the work of Berthélémy.

The Opéra tried to keep up with London and Milan in imitation of their neoclassic designs. One of the most important neoclassical choreographers, Salvatore Viganò, came from Italy and worked all over Europe, in London, Vienna, and his native Milan. His name, as well as his wife's, appear in the programs for Dauberval's ballets in London during the 1790–92 seasons. Viganò collaborated with the exceptional designer Alessandro Sanquirico (1777–1849). At La Scala in Milan their work became the focal point of the ideals of neoclassicism. The stage picture was grand, ordered and calm, while Viganò s choreography portrayed heroic and elaborate historical spectacles. Massive theatrical effects accompanied the rhythmic pantomime telling the ancient Roman stories of *I Titani* and *La Vestale* (Clark and Crisp 1978: 68).

Illustrations of Viganò drawn by J. G. Schadow display his costume of white, close-fitting breeches (aristocratic) and a light, short-sleeved coat with flared skirts. The coat is pale blue or deep pink, lined with white and bound with a white sash tied in a bow at the back so as to leave flowing ends. There is a relaxed, light, and flowing quality to the style. In another drawing, we see Viganò and his wife, Marie Medina. She wears Greek sandals and has a transparent dress gathered beneath the breasts and looks quite naked compared to Viganò who is partnering her (Beaumont 1946: 29). Viganò s carefully choreographed rhythmic interpretation of Italian myth and history centers him as one of the counterfeiters of the neoclassical tradition in Europe.[4]

Another capable designer of Italian origin, Vincenzio Sestini, the King's Theatre costumier, was initially a singer married to the well-known soprano Giovanna Sestini. He first became a tailor, then a costumier, renowned for his neoclassic opera and ballet designs. He created dresses for the ballets *Venus and Adonis* (1793), *Iphigenia in Aulide* (1793), Mme Hilligsberg's benefit (1794), *L'Amour et Psiche* (1796), *Sappho and Phaon* (1797), and *Alessandro e Timotes* (1800). He also designed a costume parody for the caricature engraving by Thomas Rowlandson in 1791, "The Prospect Before Us" which depicted members of the King's theatre company begging in the streets. Among those in the picture are Mme Hilligsberg and "Poor Old Servini," a nickname or a mistake for Sestini, since no one by the name of Servini is known to have been with the King's company at that time.

Important changes in footwear also affected the way in which both the social and the professional dancer moved. The dancing shoe of minuets, waltzes, and quadrilles rapidly became the ballet slipper and standard apparel for preparatory classes. Some dance historians, for example, Marion Hannah Winter and Ivor Guest, alluded to the fact that rope dancers wore soft shoes for balancing and that the ballet dancers of the late eighteenth century imitated this practice. The gradual change from high heel to lower heel to sandal to slipper and finally to pointe shoe seemed completely within the concept of how women's feet looked to society, regardless of their natural shape. (See also rope dancers in illustrations for M. H. Winter's *Theatre of Marvels*, and M. F. Christout's *Le Merveilleux et le Thâ tre du Silence.*)

Despite discomforts, satin or silk slippers provided flexibility for the foot and enhanced the possibilities for jumping, balancing, and turning. For example, when making a *demi-coupé* and stepping onto a *demi-pointe*, the foot takes a shape where with an enforced arch or instep, the toes are extended as well, making the foot arch and point so that the line of the leg becomes much longer and vertical. These are directives about which Gennaro Magri wrote in his 1779 treatise. Gradually the foot became more than a balancing device to help shift the weight, it became a mechanical tool or organ that could be strengthened, exercised, and expanded in its own right. And this is exactly what began to happen in

Judith Chazin-Bennahum

Figure 11
The Bishop of Durham takes a good look! © Copyright The British Museum.

the latter part of the eighteenth century, but could not really evolve until the foot was freed from the heel, however high it was (Magri 1988).

The fame and beauty of female ballet soloists spread throughout the large cities of Western Europe and brought increasing attention to the development of their virtuosic and dramatic capabilities, one outdoing the other. The neoclassic costume contributed to their renown. Mlle Parisot shocked London audiences in 1796 with her high legs flying in the ballet *le Triomphe de l'Amour*. *The Monthly Mirror* (October 1796) cited Parisot's flexibility that "created a stir by raising her legs far higher than was customary for dancers." In 1798, the Bishop of Durham made an example of her immoral moves and denounced her in an intemperate speech before the House of Lords. Subsequently, the opera administration changed the colors of dancers' maillots from flesh colored to white. (Swift 1974: 98)

At the time of the Revolution, the changing neoclassic costume, as well as a more enlightened view of dance as an expressive art, contributed to the growth of popularity in the ballet-pantomime or *ballet d'action*. It may have been the soft, flat slipper or the light textiles or the maskless face or the wigless head, but more than any other change in the quality of its dancing, ballet abandoned the steppy sequences of Baroque forms and took to the air, to the notion of height, length and grandeur of movement, and began to flow more freely covering the whole stage (Bennahum 1988: 168).

Notes

1. See Aileen Ribeiro's *The Art of Dress: Fashion in England and France, 1750–1820,* 1996.
2. See June Swann's study *Shoes.* London: Batsford, 1982, 1984.
3. This description was mentioned in an exhibition at the British Museum, April 1996, that dealt with Sir William Hamilton's work and his Emma.
4. Anyone wishing to understand the full splendor of Milanese design in the early years of the nineteenth century is referred to the *Raccolto di Scene Teatrali eseguite o disgnate d'al piu celebri Pittori Scenici,* Milano, a collection of 194 settings edited by Stanislas Stucchi and published in 1830. These include no fewer than 117 settings by Sanquirico. See also Winter 1962, 1974.

References

Beaumont, Cyril. 1946. *Beaumont Ballet Design, Past and Present.* London: The Studio and New York: Studio Publications.

Bennahum, Judith Chazin. 1988. *Dance in the Shadow of the Guillotine.* Carbondale, IL: Southern Illinois University Press.

Boucher, François. 1983. *Histoire du Costume en Occident.* Paris: Flammarion.

Browne, Alice. 1987. *The Eighteenth Century Feminist Mind.* Brighton, Sussex: The Harvester Press.

Christout, Marie-Françoise. 1965. *Le Merveilleux et le Thâ tre du Silence.* Paris: Editions Moulon, La Haye.

Clark, Mary and Crisp, Clement. 1978. *Design for Ballet.* London: Studio Vista.

Delpierre, Madeleine. 1997. *Dress in France in the Eighteenth Century.* Trans. Caroline Beamish. New Haven, CT and London: Yale University Press.

Ewing, Elizabeth. 1971. *Fashion in Underwear.* London: B. T. Batsford Ltd.

—— . 1984. *Everyday Dress: 1650–1900.* London: B. T. Batsford Ltd.

Falcone, Francesca. 1996. "The Arabesque." *Dance Chronicle* 19 (3), 231–53.

Guest, Ivor. 1996. *The Ballet of the Enlightenment.* London: Dance Books, Cecil Court.

Hollander, Anne. 1993. *Seeing Through Clothes.* Berkeley, CA: University of California Press.

Laver, James. 1995. *Costume and Fashion.* London: Thames & Hudson.

Magri, Gennaro. 1988. *Theoretical and Practical Treatise on Dancing,* Naples 1779. Trans. Mary Skeaping, London. Dance Books, Cecil Court.

Porter, James I. (ed.) 1999. *Constructions of the Classical Body*. Ann Arbor, MI: University of Michigan Press.

Ribeiro, Aileen. 1983. *Visual History of Costume in the Eighteenth Century*. London: B. T. Batsford, Drama Book Publishers.

—— . 1996. *The Art of Dress: Fashion in England and France, 1750–1820*. New Haven, CT: Yale University Press.

Sandoz, Marc. 1979. *Jean Simon Berthélemy*. Paris: Editart.

Squire, Geoffrey. 1974. *Dress, Art and Society*. London: Studio Vista.

Starobinski, Jean. 1988. *1789: Emblems of Reason*. Trans. Barbara Bray. Cambridge, MA: MIT Press.

Swann, June. 1982, 1984. *Shoes*. London: Batsford.

Swift, Mary Grace. 1974. *A Loftier Flight: The Life and Accomplishments of Charles-Louis Didelot Balletmaster*. Middletown, CT: Wesleyan University Press.

Winter, Marian Hannah. 1962. *Le Thâ tre du Merveilleux*. Paris: Olivier Perrin.

—— . 1974. *Pre-Romantic Ballet*. New York: Dance Horizons.

Fashion Theory, Volume 6, Issue 4, pp. 387–420
Reprints available directly from the Publishers.
Photocopying permitted by licence only.

Matrona and Whore: The Clothing of Women in Roman Antiquity[1]

Kelly Olson

Kelly Olson is Assistant Professor of Classical Studies at the University of Western Ontario, London, Canada. She is currently at work on a book-length study of female clothing and adornment in ancient Rome, entitled *Fashioning the Female in Roman Antiquity.*

Clothing is an important part of the sign system of every society, a central aspect of its visual language. Clothing has the power to express rank, communicate status, wealth, and power, express the relation between the sexes, reflect values, exemplify anxieties. The dress behavior of any society has everything to do with gestures, sexuality, hygiene, economics, rituals, signs, morality, and law. Clothing therefore embodies social structure and is important to a society's sense of itself. Philippe Perrot has noted that clothing in the ancien régime in France served as a sign system, a code, with its own language and purpose: to render visible the social hierarchy (Perrot 1994: 8–10, 16). Clothing was therefore an important tool of social regulation since it was a system of signs that reflected and even helped construct the social order (Perrot 1994: 8, 10, 15). Is what Perrot says in regard to clothing in the ancien régime also (with caution) applicable to antiquity?

Clothing's socio-political function in other pre-industrial societies had the effect of reinforcing the social hierarchy in them, and symbolized "self-affirmation for some and subordination for others, freezing everyone in their place by guaranteeing the place of everyone" (Perrot 1994: 10) and at first glance this also appears true for Roman antiquity. But although Roman clothing was at once the sign and the generator of rank and status, such symbols in a highly mobile society (within particular boundaries)[2] like that of Rome did not render the social structure immobile. This article suggests not so much that there was usurpation of the clothing of different ranks in Roman antiquity (which is common knowledge to historians of Roman male clothing and symbols of status), but that the *deliberate* omission of the distinctive garments that marked one's own rank might be more common than previously suspected (*contra*, e.g., Garnsey and Saller 1987: 116–17).[3] In addition, there was enough overlap among sartorial boundaries that clothing distinctions were probably not as immutable and as steadfast as authors (ancient and modern) would have us believe. This blurring of vestimentary (and consequently social) boundaries is especially evident in an examination of female dress in Roman antiquity; specifically the dress of the married woman (*matrona*) and prostitute.

I have tried to restrict the spatial and temporal parameters of this article to the women of Italy, mainly (but not exclusively) those in Rome itself, during the central period in Roman history; that is, roughly 200 BC to AD 200 (Bradley 1994: xi, 6; Brunt 1988: 9–12). Space precludes any detailed study of the women of the provinces. The problems which the male-authored literary sources present for the study of ancient women are well-known;[4] and, as one author has stated, "even these élite voices are somewhat disparate in their distribution in time and space" (Flemming 1999: 40). Also, when the historian speaks of "Rome" and "Roman society," she refers "at one extreme to a single city in Italy and at the other extreme to the whole of the empire. The shift is one of a geographical to a cultural designation, from the city in a narrow sense to wherever the city's culture came to impose itself" (Bradley: 1994, 6). Thus I have used as "Roman" evidence a number of distinct sources which I believe reflect something of the social history and cultural mores of this period: the predictable satirists and epigrammists, but also moralists, historians, later lexicographers, and antiquarians, even Greek romances written in the Roman period.[5] Most certainly follow the expected conventions of their particular genre (Ovid the love poet tends to encourage women to adorn themselves, for instance; Seneca the moralist tends to oppose it), but where the sources intrigue and attract the scholar is in their lines of intersection and correlation, in their points of consensus concerning female clothing and the adorned woman.

Naturally, any study of Roman clothing and responses to it will want to make use of the wealth of artistic material available. While the nature of Roman art is certainly "public and status-oriented" (Stone 1995: 21) and never merely a snapshot of everyday life, this type of evidence may still prove useful for the historian. The ideals of costume present in Roman literature are, often, not those which visual sources offer (and vice versa)—an interesting disjunction, if one may assume Roman art reflects the way Romans wished to be perceived.

Clothing and Roman Social Hierarchies

Roman male clothing especially was intended to indicate the social hierarchy, and there were specific sartorial signals meant to designate each order (senators, knights, the free poor, and slaves). The most common type of usurpation of status symbols occurred in relation to the rank of *eques* or knight, because equestrian rank was personal, not hereditary (see Reinhold 1971: 281, 285). Usurpation of equestrian symbols of rank seems to have been widespread in the Imperial period, and ancient sources tell of men illegally wearing expensive purple garments, particularly the *angustus clavus* (the narrow stripe on the tunic which marked the *eques*) and the gold ring: clearly, the Romans understood that the right to wear certain distinctive symbols was inherent in the acquisition of rank. Interestingly, the privileges marked by these insignia were privileges of prestige and status only: no money or political benefits accrued to the usurpers. In AD 22, a *senatus consultum* (a decree of the Senate) was passed forbidding the usurpation of equestrian status symbols; from then on three generations of free birth and 400,000 sesterces were required to wear the narrow stripe and ring. "Subsequently," Pliny the Elder remarked, "people began to apply in crowds for this mark of rank," noting that even freedmen were assuming the status.[6] The casual observer would not be able to tell who was a *iustus eques* and who was not, or whether the gorgeously dressed man with the large retinue had just pawned a ring to buy his dinner. "For it is clear that sight does not always produce true effects; indeed, the mind is frequently deceived by visual judgments," Vitruvius wrote.[7] Usurpation of senatorial symbols of status was rare (the senatorial order was smaller), but we do hear (through Martial) of an audacious ex-slave who sat in the front row of seats sporting garments of Tyrian purple and the senator's distinctive red shoeboots ornamented with the *luna* or crescent, and (through Juvenal) of one enterprising man who sewed the crescent of the senator onto his black shoe.[8]

But besides cases of usurpation of symbols of rank not one's own, there were other, more significant, instances of deviance from ideal or expected appearance in Roman antiquity, in which symbols of status or rank were left off entirely (surprising in such an apparently status-conscious society). The mark of the male citizen was supposedly the toga, but poorer men (free and freed) would not necessarily have owned one, since the toga was expensive, hard to care for, hot, and cumbersome: Tacitus refers to the *plebs* contemptuously as "the tunic-clad populace." But Augustus had to legislate in order to ensure that even the upper classes wore the toga, and Martial and Juvenal both testify to the garment's unpopularity.[9] Leaving off the toga may have led to a certain amount of sartorial confusion. There was, for instance, a natural correlation between the clothing of the slave and his low social position (there are references in the sources to "slave dress"), but no clothes associated with slavery particularly. K. R. Bradley points out that because the toga was assumed by free men mainly on formal occasions, and because slaves at Rome had no special racial characteristics, the appearance of the toga-less poor (or even middling) free was likely to be confused with that of slaves.[10]

So, although male clothing offered a series of signs that indicated the social order, it did not necessarily strengthen that order: sartorial signs were illicitly usurped or even tacitly omitted, and there were gaps between rank and the vestimentary signs of rank. Because it was hard to enforce legislation concerning status symbols, and because many of them were a function of wealth, vestimentary and other signs served to visualize the social hierarchy but not necessarily to reinforce it. It has been said that restrictions on the usurpation of status symbols particular to a class are designed as an attempt to enforce social boundaries; however, legislation designed to stop this practice in Rome "was simply not enforced systematically" (Reinhold 1971: 276). Thus dress at Rome could produce confusion, rather than clarification, of social boundaries.

Nonetheless, rank was conceived by the Romans as including the right to wear certain articles of clothing (as is evident in cases of usurpation of equestrian and senatorial status symbols), whether or not these articles were actually assumed: often an article of clothing or ornament came to symbolize the office or legal status and its power, whatever the sartorial reality. The Latin language thus employed the outward sign of status or rank, such as an article of clothing, to stand in for the status or rank itself. For instance, the right to stand for office was termed the right of the *latus clavus* (the wide stripe on a magistrate's toga), incorporation into the rank of *eques* the *ius anuli aurei* (the "right of the gold ring"). Even the phrase *calceos mutare* ("to change into shoeboots") meant "to become a senator."[11]

That clothing was viewed by the Romans as part of a moral system as well as part of the outward arrangement of visualizing rank is not a new discovery, and is, in fact, the main focus of much recent scholarship on ancient clothing.[12] Since the Romans equated oddities in dress with oddities of behavior, Quintilian (for instance) has many cautions and recommendations on the proper cut and draping of an orator's toga: improper draping could harm a career (Stone 1995: 17). Quintilian insisted that the tunic must fall to just below the knees, "since only women draw them lower and centurions higher;" care must be taken to see that the purple stripe, falls in the correct way, "since negligence sometimes is noted."[13] To wrap the toga about oneself in the heat of speaking was a sign "almost of madness," to throw it over the right shoulder effeminate, but to neglect to rearrange a slipped toga near the beginning of one's speech was a sign of "indifference, or sloth, or ignorance of the way in which clothes ought to be worn." But conversely, "excessive care with regard to the toga, the shoes, or the hair, is just as reprehensible as excessive carelessness,"[14] as it could make the wearer seem effeminate and un-Roman.

Female dress was equally supposed to indicate a woman's rank, status, and morality. The sources present more difficulties for the study of female clothing, inasmuch as the ancient authors tend to mention male (rather than female) clothing when they mention it at all. Still, some useful information may be gleaned from literary references. *Matronae*, the wives of Roman citizens, are said to wear the *stola* (a long slip-like garment worn over the underdress or tunic).[15] The *stola* first and foremost indicated that the wearer was married in a *iustum matrimonium* (a legal marriage between two citizens) and it was therefore a mark of honor, a way to distinguish sexual and social rank in broad fashion. Literary sources also tell us that Roman women wore the *palla* or mantle, which was drawn over the head when out of doors, and bound their hair with woolen bands or fillets.[16] This description is offered by several modern scholars as that of the everyday clothing of the Roman *matrona*.[17]

Close inspection of both literary sources and the visual record, however, shows that women (as with men and the toga) apparently did not always assume these signs of rank and status. For example, according to one (admittedly not entirely trustworthy) source, by the second half of the second century there was an increasing inclination among women of the upper classes to abandon the *stola*[18] (wives of the poorest citizens likely would not have worn the *stola* since, like the toga, it would have been an uncomfortable hindrance to manual labor, another possible instance of the omission of a status symbol). The *stola* seems to have had a relatively short lifespan in comparison to its male counterpart the toga: the earliest artistic portrayal of a woman in a *stola* is dated to the early first century BC, but the overwhelming majority of stolate busts and statues are Julio-Claudian, and *stolae* do not appear to be in evidence after the time of Faustina Minor (d. AD 175).[19] The toga, in comparison, existed as a garment (albeit largely ceremonial) until the fifth century (Stone 1995: 38). Nor does every woman in the artistic record wear a *stola*, which we would expect if the garment was the essential and quotidian status symbol the literary sources describe. As for the *palla*, the vast majority of female portrait busts we possess show the woman with an unveiled head (probably in order to display her elaborate hairstyle to the viewer).[20] It is difficult to see how most of these architectural hairstyles could have withstood a mantle being laid on top without crushing the rows of curls and braids. Even in the Ara Pacis procession (Figure 1), an outdoor and

Figure 1
Ara Pacis Procession.
© Deutsches Archäolog.
Institut, 72.2403.

public scene and one of Augustan date, where we would expect to find all the women with the *palla* drawn up around their heads,[21] some are veiled, and some are not: apparently it was a decision left to the discretion of a woman. And although mentioned several times in the literary sources, except for busts of Vestal Virgins, and some of women sacrificing, there are few portraits in which the woman is actually portrayed with her hair tied in fillets. It is clear that not every woman wore them, or perhaps wore them only on religious or ceremonial occasions.[22] Again, it is hard to see what place they could occupy on the head if the woman chose to wear an elaborate hairstyle.

There is some disjunction, then, between the literary and the artistic sources for the costume of the Roman woman. The combination of *stola, palla,* and fillets, by no means ubiquitous in portrait busts, statues, and reliefs, was very strongly linked with the appearance of the honorable married woman in literary sources: "be far from here, you signs of purity, thin *vittae* and long *stola* (*instita*) which covers the feet," says Ovid.[23] These "signs of purity" are seldom found in the visual record, very likely because much of what we read in ancient literature about women's clothing seems to be prescriptive. The literary record describes what the *matrona* should look like and how her clothing should embody her moral stance; she seems to be described in terms of exemplary (not actual) appearance. Martial, for instance, instead of employing a long phrase which delineates a specific social rank and accompanying moral probity, simply names articles of clothing: "whoever he be, despiser of *stola* or purple, that has assailed with verses those whom he ought to respect." A woman clearly did not have to wear these vestimentary signs in order to be associated with them.[24]

It is not my intention to give a description of every garment in Roman society that was designed to indicate rank or status, and to speculate whether (or on which occasions) such a garment was actually assumed. I will state again, however, that literary description of sartorial boundaries seems to represent ideal or prescribed costume, and that the omission of signs of rank and status, as opposed to the assumption of signs of a status not one's own by law, may have been more common than scholars have supposed. Rome was a finely graded society with social mobility within particular boundaries; thus our elite authors display a fierce concern with *insignia dignitatis* and the regulation of symbols of rank. But clothing and status did not always necessarily correspond: what authors in general describe is an ideal sartorial situation, in which all citizens wear the toga, all *equites* the gold ring, all married women the *stola*, no one ornaments himself above his status, and the social order is both immediately apparent and, ultimately, immutable.

The Prostitute

In Roman antiquity prostitutes and adulteresses too were presumably immediately identifiable from their clothing: both wore the toga. By this "exclusion" from the sartorial distinctions of the chaste *matronae*, the toga ideally identified them as those who rejected the moral code bound up in those clothes. Specific passages on the togate woman are few, and may be quoted here.[25]

The following authors link the toga with an adulteress or a woman whose status is uncertain:

1. Martial berates a friend for giving a notorious adulteress (*famosa moecha*) dresses of purple and scarlet. "Do you want to give her the present she has deserved? Send her the toga."[26]
2. Martial elsewhere bestows the epithet *damnata moecha* (possibly "a convicted [?] adulteress") on the eunuch Thelys, who wears a toga.[27]
3. Juvenal complains of an effeminate advocate's gauzy toga: "Fabulla is an adulteress; condemn Carfinia of the same crime if you wish; but however guilty, she would never wear such a gown as yours."[28] Possibly, too, one or both women are convicted adulteresses (hence the adjective *damnata*).
4. Martial criticizes a man as being the son of a woman who wore the toga—*mater togata* (there is no specification otherwise as to her status).[29]
5. Horace mentions a *togata* (possibly an *ancilla togata*) and elsewhere states the *togata* has the advantage over the *matrona* when it comes to satisfying sexual urges, as there is no husband to fear[30] (there is no specification as to the social status of the *togata*).
6. Porphyrio wrote that "women who were convicted of having committed adultery were forced to go out in public togate."[31]

There are a few authors who associate the toga specifically with the whore:

1. Cicero says to Antony "you assumed the *toga virilis* and at once turned it into the toga of a woman (*muliebrem togam*). At first you were a common whore (*scortum*), with a fixed price for your favours, nor was it small."[32]
2. Sulpicia bemoans the fact that Cerinthus is unfaithful to her, and with a prostitute: "you attend rather to the toga and to the whore loaded with a wool basket than to Sulpicia daughter of Servius."[33]
3. Nonius quotes the comic writer Titinius who also emphatically names the toga as the garment of the whore. "Even shelter can be described as a toga. Titinius in his *Gemina*: 'if he decides to head out of town with the whore, I want the keys hidden immediately, so that there be no chance for him of any undercover business in the country;' that is, no chance of shelter."[34]
5. [Acro] schol. Hor. 1.2.63: "Matrons who have been repudiated by their husbands on account of adultery lay aside the *stola* and wear the toga on account of disgrace; the toga of a prostitute is apt. For thus they are accustomed to stand forth in dark togas only, so as to be distinguished from matrons; and for that reason those women who were convicted of adultery wear this garment. In other words, women because of <a conviction for> adultery are said to go out in public togate. Others call a freedwoman togate, because previously freedwomen wore the toga, but matrons wore the *stola*."[35]

There are two problems here quite apart from the question of the normal dress of the whore. The first is the status of the woman referred to by the adjective *togata*.[36] In these passages, Martial and Juvenal speak specifically of the togate adulteress, Cicero, Nonius, Sulpicia [Tibullus], and the scholiast on Horace of the togate prostitute, but it is often unclear whether in fact a convicted adulteress or a whore is actually being referred to. When Martial calls an enemy the son of a *mater togata*, for instance, does he mean a whore or an adulteress? Horace's *togata*, again, wears transparent Coan silk and shows her body off to viewers—but the status of the woman is not specified.[37] It seems possible that in many cases *moecha* (adulteress) or *meretrix/scortum* (whore) is not indicated perhaps because they are the same type of woman in our authors' minds (i.e., sexually licentious: an adulteress was presumably generous with her sexual favors), and thus whore and adulteress did not therefore need to be distinguished absolutely.[38] An adulteress *was* a whore; this is brought out clearly in Augustus' legislation on prostitutes and adulteresses. If he did not prosecute her for adultery, the husband of a guilty wife could himself be prosecuted for pimping.[39]

Secondly, there is no specific evidence in these passages that the adulteress or the prostitute was "compelled" to wear the toga, as is often asserted by modern authors.[40] The presence of *damnata* in Martial *Epig.* 10.52 and Juvenal, and *convicta* in the scholiasts on Horace does hint at this, but there is no extant Roman law stating that assumption of the toga was part of the penalty for a *matrona*'s conviction of prostitution; nor is there any edict that states that a common whore had to wear the toga, even if she registered with the aediles as such (presumably such a regulation, if it existed, would have been enforced with the help of interested third parties).[41] Nor (*contra* [Acro]) is there any evidence in classical literature that associates the toga with freedwomen, or that states prostitutes were accustomed to wear dark togas.[42]

It is one contention of this study that the toga was not in fact the "normal" dress of the whore, but only one of many types of dress prostitutes could adopt. Although this has been stated by Thomas McGinn,[43] an account of the descriptive details of prostitute clothing is lacking, and needs to be provided comprehensively. There are many passages in classical literature in which whores, depending on their station, appear in everything from rich clothing all the way down to little (or no) clothing at all: passages in which, moreover, the toga as their distinctive dress is not named. Agorastocles in Plautus' *Poenulus* wants to delight his eyes with the "elegance of the prostitutes." Another Plautine character admires a harlot's appearance: "but the way she was dressed, bejewelled, ornamented—so charmingly, so tastefully, so stylishly!" Seneca makes reference to a harlot "adorned for the public" and "dressed in the clothes her pimp had provided." He also speaks of "whores' colors" (probably referring to make-up or bright clothing) and says that these would not be worn by decent women. He does not mention the toga. Tacitus too described the clothing of whores as colorful; again, the toga, the prostitute's supposed identifying mark, is not named.[44] Nonius states that in olden times (*apud veteres*) whores wore short tunics which were "girded up from below," and cites Afranius for an instance in which prostitutes would don long dresses: " A prostitute in a long gown?' 'When they find themselves in a strange place they tend to wear it for self-protection.'"[45] Isidore states that the clothing of a prostitute is in fact the *amiculum* or linen *pallium* (possibly a mantle which could be draped around the body). He also states that "in olden days" (*apud veteres*) adulterous matrons would wear this garment instead of a *stola*; but in his own Spain the *pallium* is conversely the mark of respectability. His vagueness is unhelpful for the study of prostitute clothing but "may be taken as a sign that the woman's toga had long since disappeared from the scene" (McGinn 1998: 167, with notes).[46] Evanthius mentions a saffron-colored *pallium* as the distinguishing mark of a prostitute in comedy.[47] In the Greek novel of Xenophon of Ephesus, the slave girl Anthia is forced to exhibit herself in front of the brothelkeeper's establishment wearing beautiful clothing and loaded with gold jewelry.[48] Some prostitutes would wear foreign headgear such as turbans to make themselves stand out and thus to increase a customer's interest. Messalina gilded her nipples and wore a blonde wig on her nightly shifts in the brothel. Well-dressed harlots could even travel in sedans, and some would dye or perfume their hair as well, to add to their allure.[49] Whores may not always have worn the *strophium* or breastband (an undergarment): one of Catullus' prostitutes suddenly bares her naked breasts to a passerby, surely indicating she was not dressed in one.[50] Nudity was the marker of the lowest whore, a woman who was said to be "ready for every kind of lust." The whores in a squalid brothel would also be naked, and Juvenal describes this sort of harlot as "the whore that stands naked in a reeking archway."[51] But there were apparently different categories of "nudity": Cicero, in claiming that Anthony was seen in public *nudus,* means he was simply going about bare-chested. This raises the possibility that Rome's streetwalkers and brothel workers were not entirely naked but merely wore clothing which did not cover them completely.[52] Tertullian and Ulpian, two sources which speak of prostitutes, do not name the toga as the whore's distinctive garment (McGinn 1998: 163). Unfortunately, there is to my knowledge no visual evidence for the dress of the Roman prostitute,[53] but the literary sources present us with a range of prostitute clothing (from rich accoutrements all the way down to nothing), which seem to have varied according to the woman's station within a hierarchy of prostitutes, and none of these sources mentions the toga. Why not?

Roman male clothing, as we have seen, had a legal basis: symbols of rank were incorporated into garments, and therefore dress was supposed to be an act of political and social signification. Ideally, social role and status could be read instantly in dress. Also, the Latin language thus often employed the outward sign of status or rank, such as an article of clothing, to stand in for the status or rank itself. Thus, the *matrona* and her moral stance were frequently specified simply by the words *stola* or *stolata* or *vittae*. Although *stola, palla,* and *vittae* do not always appear in the visual record, the *matrona* nonetheless continues to be indicated in ancient literature in terms of her ideal appearance, both because the authors do not describe but prescribe, and because such brief designations function as literary shorthand.

Likewise, it seems possible that the word *togata* was employed not to designate common social practice, but as metonomy for the sexually licentious woman. The adulteress or whore can be designated as *togata* whether or not she is actually togate: it is not a tangible piece of clothing which is indicated by the adjective, but a moral system. The device of naming an outward sign of status was employed instead of a description of that status: *togata* described in one word a woman whose morals were easy, just as *stolata* described in one word the woman who possessed a high degree of exemplary virtue. At some point in Rome's past (unfortunately now irretrievable) whores probably did wear the toga: hence its reputation as the dress of the whore. But the sources demonstrate that there was a range of prostitute clothing, and although several ancient authors mention the toga as the distinctive garment of the whore, there is sufficient evidence to state that this was only one garment that whores could adopt. Thus the use of the word *togata* to describe a woman of easy morals may not necessarily have been a token of its currency (*contra* McGinn 1998: 163). Stereotypes had, as today, only a limited basis in reality.

Matron and Whore

If they did not always wear the toga, how were prostitutes visually marked? Ancient authors from all periods and genres are adamant that whores and matrons were sartorially distinct and immediately distinguishable from one another. When one of Plautus' prostitutes is required to disguise herself as a *matrona*, for instance, she is ordered to be "dressed in the matron's way, with hair combed and tied with woolen bands so that she can pretend to be your wife." Two hundred years or so later, Ovid distinguishes between the dress of Latin brides and mothers (*vittae* and the long gown) and that of others (*vos*) who do not wear these garments. Martial asks, "who brings garments into Flora's festival and permits prostitutes the modesty of the *stola*?"[54] A *Digest* text states a woman dressed as a whore or slave laid herself open to pestering:

> If someone accost virgins, even those in slaves' garb, his offense is regarded as venial, even more so if women are in prostitutes' dress and not that of matrons. Still, if a woman is not in the dress of a matron and someone accosts her or abducts her attendant, he will be liable to the action for insult.[55] (M. Antistius Labeo [d. AD 10–22])

These passages indicate that matrons and whores were ideally sartorially distinct from one another but also strongly imply that such was not always the case.[56] And, for what it is worth, Labeo was a lawyer of Augustan date, a time in which old-fashioned clothing distinctions were supposedly of great importance. Perhaps the visual markers of whores and matrons were not quite as clear-cut as literary sources would have us think. The *Digest* passage does not specifically mention the toga as a prostitute's garment,[57] and also incidentally implies that not every matron wore the dress of a matron: and confusion results when social and sartorial boundaries are muddled.

There were other ways in which the supposedly clear vestimentary signs of matron and whore were confused: we read in the literary sources that some kinds of ornament were common to both types of women. Both whores and matrons used cosmetics, for example.[58] The use of make-up in early nineteenth-century America conventionally marked two extreme social boundaries: prostitutes and rich noblewomen. Whores tended to set trends in fashion and make-up which were often carefully toned down and employed by fashionable upper-class women.[59] This aping of prostitute fashion by women of the upper classes may also have been true in antiquity: "you have not been perverted by the imitation of worse women that leads even the virtuous into pitfalls," says Seneca to his mother (this passage occurs in the section in which he is speaking of female adornment).[60] In addition to make-up, both whores and matrons wore colored clothing.[61] In regard to the clothing of fashionable women, Plautus mentions sky-blue (*caesicius*), marigold-yellow (*caltulus*), red-orange (*crocotulus*), sea-blue (*cumatilis*), walnut brown (*carinus*), and waxy or pale yellow (*cerinus*) as female colors.[62] Ovid, writing two hundred years later, suggests instead colors that complement the complexion: sky-blue (*aer*), sea-blue (*unda*), golden (*aureus*), yellow (*croceus*), wax-yellow or pale yellow (*cereus*), dark green (*Paphiae myrti*), amethyst (*purpurae amethysti*), pale pink (*albentes rosae*), gray (*pullus*), acorn or dark brown (*glandes*), and almond-colored or beige (*amygdala*). And there are many more colors, he says, that he could name, as many as the flowers that bloom in the spring.[63] Apuleius speaks of a woman's "brightly-colored robe" (*vestis florida*), and women's clothes are often spoken of as *versicolori*, of many colors.[64] Some authors did not consider purple seemly for women, probably because of the strong status implications involved.[65] Certain lurid colors, like greenish-yellow (*galbinus*) and cherry-red (*cereus*) were deemed lower-class (at least by the elite), and Fortunata appears in them in Petronius' *Satyricon*. The girdle of Apuleius' slave-girl Photis is *russeus*, bright-red, another low hue. Elsewhere, a bright greenish-blue dinner dress (*prasinus synthesis*) is given to a mistress.[66]

A popular fabric for both classes of women was the daring Coan silk (or some imitation of it), a diaphanous stuff that apparently left little to the viewer's imagination. Seneca congratulated his mother Helvia for not having worn it: "never have you fancied the kind of dress that exposed no greater nakedness by being removed."[67] While it is possible that his distaste for the fabric might be seen as relational (i.e., unseemly on his mother but admirable on a mistress), elsewhere Seneca raged against Coan silk without naming any wearers specifically:

> I see clothing of silk, if that can be called clothing, in which there is nothing by which the body, or indeed modesty, could be protected, so that, when a woman wears it, she can scarcely swear that she is not naked.[68]

Seneca, a Roman moralist, despised the fabric, but others were full of praise for its sensual qualities. Coan silk was the notorious fabric of a woman of easy morals. "In her Coan silk you may see [the sexually licentious woman] almost as if naked," Horace reminds his readers.[69] The color and weight of a woman's clothing was ideally a reflection of her morality, and the fashion for Coan silk among upper-class women, whether truly transparent or simply an extremely thin material which outlined the body,[70] confused sartorial and therefore moral and social boundaries. It put a woman's body on display, an act that was equated with prostitution (see below).

Both classes of women also had access to jewelry: noblewomen of course, but Juvenal described a woman of humble station "who displays a long gold chain around her neck," and Pliny the Elder noted that plebeian women wore *compedes* (bracelets) of silver. Elsewhere, he notes the demand (real or imagined) for pearls by women of the lower classes.[71] These are likely not instances of peasant women wearing their dowries or wealth on their bodies (see Courtney 1980: 340 [at Juv. *Sat.* 6.589], with references) but of gold- or silver-plated ornaments, which lower-class women wore in imitation of elite status symbols. Even gems could be imitated by means of colored glass for realistic renderings of emeralds, opals, carbuncles, topazes, and sapphires.[72] Intriguingly, a late source (the *Codex Theodosianus*, AD 438) prohibited actresses from wearing gems, embroidered silks, or clothing picked out in gold. Presumably such ornamentation was thought inappropriate for their low status, which stemmed from the fact that they displayed themselves on stage and were suspected of practicing prostitution. Actresses wearing finery thus devalued the ornaments of upper-class matrons who rightfully wore them. But the same law (although how the legislation would have actually been enforced is problematic) did allow actresses to wear "checkered and varicolored silks and gold without gems on their necks, arms, and girdles."[73] Although a late source, it corroborates what earlier sources have to say about lower-class women wearing jewelry.

It seems then that comparable kinds of feminine adornment could be used by both noblewomen and whores (certainly in varying degrees, but our authors do not acknowledge this). According to moralists, cosmetics and other adornment made a woman look seductive and served merely to invite male attention (the face of such a woman, states Seneca, was proof of her shamelessness). Because, for the ancients, clothing and adornment functioned as part of a moral system, and because *matronae* and prostitutes employed similar types of ornament, authors assert that they are often unable to tell the difference between a whore and a respectable woman. The Christian Tertullian in his *De Pallio* goes further and claims that the late second century AD noblewomen were going about in public without the *stola* for the purposes of practising prostitution more easily.[74] Matrons discarded these garments ("the indices and guardians of *dignitas*," says Tertullian, though whether of husband or wife is not specified) to indulge in lower-class pleasures, to walk abroad, to see and be seen, and to field sexual advances. A woman cast off her modesty along with the *stola*, and thus men would approach her more easily (but, as noted above, the *stola* had probably fallen out of favor before Tertullian's time: it must have been, like the toga, long, hot, and cumbersome; women likely discarded it for reasons of comfort rather than sexual licentiousness). He also claims, more fantastically, that prostitutes in turn were adopting the clothing and markers of the upper-class woman. Clothing, says Tertullian, pre-announced character; therefore the clothing of the whores was all the more disturbing, women who "some laws formerly restrained from [the use of] matrimonial and matronly decoration; but now, the daily increasing depravity of the age has raised [these whores] to so nearly an equality with the most honorable women, that the difficulty is to distinguish between them."[75] It is unclear why wearing chaste clothing would be good for a whore's business (particularly since Tertullian had previously claimed that wearing a *stola* makes men afraid to approach a woman); certainly he is exaggerating for the rhetorical purpose of exhorting Christian women to leave off over-adorning, and may be saying too that all women are lustful and shameless (or perhaps merely implying that the signs of chastity were also the signs of the upper class, which is what led the whores to adopt them). Tertullian, like Seneca before him, displays profound anxiety because he imagines that *matronae* cannot be told from whores: for him the normal social classes are in confusion and flux; noblewoman and prostitute have been assimilated into one category.

We have seen that the hierarchy of moral behavior was thought to correspond directly with how much or what type of clothing the woman was wearing. Since a woman's clothing made visible her moral position, a woman laid aside her modesty along with her clothing: naked or scantily-clad whores would satisfy any lust. And clothing that marked a woman excessively, like Coan silk, was censured because of the perceived moral implications. "For a woman, in fact, the one glory is chastity; so she must take care to be chaste—and to be seen to be chaste," wrote Seneca.[76] Women gave advance warning of their shamelessness by dress, talk, walk, and appearance,[77] and clothing therefore constructed a social identity for the wearer at the same time as it signified that wearer's identity. The outward signs that were supposed to visualize the social order for Tertullian (and Seneca) instead perverted it; the disturbing truth was that clothing could insinuate things about the wearer that were half-truths or outright lies.

We need not posit a moral breakdown of Roman society in the late second century AD, however, in order to account for the confusion of vestimentary signs. The different styles of clothing for each class of women (the *stola* for matrons and the toga for whores) which were supposedly employed to mark rank and status, as stated, represented an ideal situation. The seeming confusion concerning the clothing of *matronae* and whores in the sources may in part stem from the fact that the adorned woman who made herself conspicuous in society and wanted to put her body on show for the visual delectation of others was often likened to a prostitute. The adorned woman ran the risk of being accosted, at the very least: "a married woman who wants to be safe from the lust of the seducer must go out dressed up (*ornata*) only so far as to avoid unkemptness (*inmunda*)."[78] More importantly, blatant and purposeful display of the self, however clothed, led to a dwindling of female modesty, and for a woman to be seen and a man to see promoted the desire for sexual relations on the part of both.[79] Propertius, for instance, claims his love for Cynthia grows stronger "by looking" (*spectando*). Having glimpsed a girl's legs, Ovid burns all the more for sexual knowledge of her; elsewhere, he becomes smitten with a girl in a portico he has seen but never conversed with.[80] Elsewhere, Ovid claims women came to the games to observe and be observed: "to chastity the place is fatal," he concludes.[81] Women supposedly became sexually excited when they put themselves on display: chastity was eroded by being seen. Therefore, the adorned woman who ornamented herself for public display was no better than a prostitute. The prostitute was often described as wheedling, cajoling, or coaxing (*blanda*) or taught to coax (*docetur blanditias*), she showed herself off in public, a notice was put above the door of the cella of the brothel whore advertising her body, and she welcomed all comers.[82] A whore was also taught to "make all kinds of movement with her body"[83] to entice men. The dressed woman was considered to do all these things on a visual level: she put herself on public display to coax attention through appearance,[84] was thought to welcome the gaze and hence the desire of men, visually advertised her willingness for sex, and used her body to attract.[85]

Conclusions

M. Reinhold wrote in 1971:

> the institutionalization of distinctive modes of dress as status symbols of class gradations, common in many cultures, did not characterize Roman society in the first few centuries of the empire, despite the intensity of class consciousness. There was never any serious intention of establishing a "hierarchy of clothing" during the Principate, not merely because of the force of tradition but also because of fear of arousing class friction (Reinhold 1971: 282).

As many scholars have noted, however, distinctive modes of dress were indeed characterized as status symbols in Roman antiquity (the gold ring and narrow stripe on the tunic of the *eques* are obvious examples) and, despite the fact that there was no established legal hierarchy of clothing, there was a system of sartorial signs which was unofficial, understood, and acknowledged. Male clothing in Roman society was supposed to delineate clearly the social rank and status of each of its members. *Iusti equites* wore the narrow purple stripe; senators the *luna*; citizens the toga. But what the ancient authors describe is an ideal vestimentary situation which corresponds to a ideal static social situation, and we can identify instances of deviance from expected appearance (the usurpation of the gold ring of the *eques*, for example, or even, more unexpectedly, the omission of the toga). The system rather encouraged the usurpation of sartorial signs and the resultant social confusion. Vestimentary rules and regulations were more fluid than the authors (who write in the main about regulatory clothing) disclose.

Much of what is said about female appearance in literary sources also seems to be prescription: what matrons wore and what prostitutes wore may not always have been completely straightforward and distinct. A woman may be described as *stolata* or *togata* not because she is stolate or togate, but because for many authors clothing indicated a moral system. Despite the firm pronouncements of the sources, appearance and status did not always necessarily correspond: the stark sartorial demarcation between whore and matron is to a certain extent a product of idealization. Matron and whore were surely distinguishable from each other on the street but perhaps not as strongly as our authors could have wished (and certainly they are also exaggerating the similarities between matron and prostitute for rhetorical purposes). That not every prostitute wore a brightly colored transparent toga nor every matron a modest *stola* is made abundantly clear by the *Digest* passage above (see p. 397). Ideal clothing is stressed precisely because the social and vestimentary categories of women in Roman antiquity were not as sharply delineated as the exemplar demanded.

Notes

1. This article is part of a larger study on women's appearance in Roman antiquity. All translations are from the Loeb Classical Library, with minor alterations. Abbreviations of ancient authors and their works may be found in S. Hornblower and A. Spawforth (eds) 1996. *The Oxford Classical Dictionary* (3rd edn). Oxford and New York: Oxford University Press. Journal abbreviations are those in *L'année philologique* (1999. Paris: Société d'édition "Les belles lettres"). I am grateful to K. R. Bradley, and R. P. Saller for commenting on earlier drafts of this article. My deepest appreciation, however, is due to *Fashion Theory*'s anonymous referee, whose rigorously precise and insightful comments saved me from error, sharpened the focus of the study, and offered significant improvements to the final version. All mistakes remain my own.

2. On social mobility in Roman antiquity, see Garnsey and Saller 1987: 123–5, who state that, although for sectors of the population the prospects of mobility were virtually hopeless, "the scale of movement among the elite orders of the Roman empire was remarkable" (p. 123).

3. The bibliography on Roman clothing is slowly growing, especially with the publication of Sebesta and Bonfante 1995, which comprises short articles on many aspects of Roman costume, including men's and

women's clothing, jewelry, shoes, and clothing in literature, and now must be regarded as the starting place for all historians of Roman costume. In this volume, see especially LaFollette 1995; Sebesta 1995a, b. Also of interest: Dyck 2001; H. R. Goette. *Studien zu römischen Togadarstellungen* (Mainz am Rhein: P. von Zabern, 1990); B. Holtheide. 1980. "*Matrona stolata—femina stolata.*" ZPE 38: 127–34; Palmer 1998; Scholz 1992; Sebesta 1997; C. Vout. 1996. "The Myth of the Toga: Understanding the History of Roman Dress." *G&R* 43.2: 204–20; L. M. Wilson, *The Roman Toga* (Baltimore, MD: Johns Hopkins University Press, 1924), and Wilson 1938.

4. On which see, for instance, V. French. 1990. "What is Central for the Study of Women in Antiquity?" *Helios* 17: 213–20.

5. Using Greek novels as a source for Roman society is controversial. But see Bradley 1994: 9, in which he states: "in their assumptions of what is plausible and credible in everyday life … these narratives reflect aspects of contemporary reality that can provide valuable historical information."

6. Pliny *HN* 33.33: *postea gregatim insigne id adpeti coeptum . . . passimque ad ornamenta ea etiam servitute liberati transiliant* (see also Suet. *Claud.* 25). On equestrian status, see P. A. Brunt, "The *Equites* in the Late Republic," in R. Seager (ed.) 1969, *The Crisis of the Roman Republic,* pp. 83–115. Cambridge: Cambridge University Press; P. A. Brunt. 1983. "*Princeps* and *equites.*" *JRS* 73: 42–75; and T. P. Wiseman. 1970. "The Definition of 'eques Romanus' in the Late Republic." *Historia* 19: 67–83. The free birth requirement also meant a rush to acquire fictive *ingenuitas,* which could be granted by imperial favor; see Reinhold 1971: 286. The *ius anuli aurei* was exclusive to *equites* and was supposed to be legally regulated, but was often granted by those in power to men below the legal rank: Verres publicly bestowed the gold ring on his clerk, for instance, much to Cicero's disgust, since neither had participated in any significant military victories (Cic. *Verr.* 2.3.185–7) and Sulla granted it to the actor Q. Roscius Gallus (Macrob. *Sat.* 3.14.3). *Equites* were ideally distinguished by a gold ring, but Augustus granted the right to wear the iron ring to a certain stratum of *equites*/jurors (Pliny *HN* 33.30); in the Republican period, certain senators wore an iron ring in private and a gold ring in public (Pliny *HN* 33.12). This is further complicated by the fact that some freedmen, and even slaves, apparently wore an iron ring plated with gold (Pliny *HN* 33.23). By AD 197 Septimius Severus granted the right to wear the gold ring to all soldiers (Herodian 3.8.4). On the *ius anuli aurei* generally, see Pliny *HN* 33. 29–33; Reinhold 1971: 285–7; and A. M. Stout, "Jewelry as a Symbol of Status in the Roman Empire," in Sebesta and Bonfante 1995: 78. Equestrian status symbols (including rings) were a subject of legislation both by Augustus (Pliny *HN* 33.30) and Tiberius (Pliny *HN* 33.32).

7. Dinner: Mart. *Epig.* 2.57; Vitr. 6.2.2: *non enim veros videtur habere visus effectus, sed fallitur saepius iudicio ab eo mens.*

8. Mart. *Epig.* 2.29; Juv. *Sat.* 7.192: *adpositam nigrae lunam subtexit alutae*; Reinhold 1971: 280. Of course, these two examples may only be general paradigms of the authors' disgust for the undeserving who rise to social prominence. See Isid. *Orig.* 19.34.4 and Stat. *Silv.* 5.2.28, who also mention the *luna*. This shoe emblem unfortunately appears nowhere in the artistic record; perhaps it was a comparatively short-lived ornament. On the textual problems of Juv. *Sat.* 7.192, see Courtney 1980: 374.

9. Tac. *Dial.* 7: *tunicatus . . . populus.* Augustus enacted legislation forcing men to assume the toga (Suet. *Aug.* 40) as part of his programme to reform public and private morality. Unpopularity: Juv. *Sat.* 3.171–2; Mart. *Epig.* 10.47.5. The toga was a garment increasingly reserved for formal or ceremonial occasions: see Stone 1995: *passim.*

10. On slave clothing generally, see Bradley 1994: 95–9, with references. Seneca (*de Clem.* 1.24.1) implies that slaves and the poor freeborn were sartorially indistinguishable.

11. On the *latus clavus*, see B. Levick. 1991. "A Note on the *latus clavus*." *Athenaeum* 79: 239–44; and R. P. Saller. 1982. *Personal Patronage Under the Early Empire*, pp. 50–2. Cambridge: Cambridge University Press. *Calceos mutare*: Cic. *Phil.* 13.13.28.

12. See L. Bonfante. 1995. "Introduction." In Sebesta and Bonfante 1995: 5; Dyck 2001; E. Gunderson. 1998. "Discovering the Body in Roman oratory." In M. Wyke (ed.), *Parchments of Gender: Deciphering the Bodies of Antiquity*, pp. 169–89. Oxford: Oxford University Press; Heskel 1995; Sebesta 1997. For cosmetics as a marker of what was undesirable in a Roman woman, see Richlin 1995 and Wyke 1994.

    Earlier studies of ancient clothing have been antiquarian, not historical, in focus: the precise shape and size of the toga, for instance, or speculations on shades of clothing dyes. Roman female clothing has been somewhat neglected: in a recent "daily life" book, for instance, the chapter entitled "Clothing" makes no mention whatsoever of female garments (F. Dupont. 1989. *Daily Life in Ancient Rome*, pp. 258–68. Trans. C. Woodall. Oxford: Oxford University Press).

13. Quint. *Instit.* 11.3.138: *nam infra mulierum est, supra centurionum*; 11.3.139: *ut purpurea recte descendat, levis cura est; notatur interim negligentia.* In a lost work, Pliny the Elder asserted that Cicero wore his toga in a fashion meant to conceal his varicose veins (Quint. *Instit.* 11.3.143).

14. Quint. *Instit.* 11.3.146: *paene furiosum est.*; Quint. *Instit.* 11.3.149: *non reponere eam prorsus negligentis aut pigri aut quomodo debeat amiciri nescientis est*; Quint. *Instit.* 11.3.137: *nam et toga et calceus et capillus tam nimia cura quam neglegentia sunt reprehendenda.*

15. Freedwomen married to Roman *ingenuii* were apparently given the right to wear the *stola* at the time of the Second Punic War; the term

is *longa vesta*, interpreted by scholars as the *stola* (Macrob. *Sat.* 1.6.13). On freedwomen and the *stola*, see Palmer 1998: 27–31. Interest in the *stola* and the morality it embodied is recent in the history of ancient costume: see Scholz 1992 (with exhaustive references); Sebesta 1995a, 1997.

16. *Palla*: Isid. *Orig.* 19.25; Val. Max. 6.3.10; Sen. *Controv.* 2.7.6; Prop. 2.23.13. Fillets: Plaut. *Miles* 790–3; Ovid *Ars* 1.31, 3.483; *Pont.* 3.3.51–2; Isid. *Orig.* 19.31.6; Val. Max. 5.2.1; Tib. 1.6.67. For fillets in the hair of young girls, see Prop. 4.11.34; Val. Flacc. 8.6; Non. 353L.

17. See for instance E. Dench. 1998. "Austerity, Excess, Success, and Failure in Hellenistic and Early Imperial Italy." In Wyke 1998 (above, n. 12): 144; Sebesta 1995a: 48–50; Sebesta 1997: 535–7; Wilson 1938: 146–62; and P. Zanker. 1988. *The Power of Images in the Age of Augustus*, pp. 165–6. Trans. A. Shapiro. Ann Arbor, MI: University of Michigan Press.

18. See Wilson 1938: 161. Tertullian, writing in the late second century, reported that certain women had left off wearing the *stola*, and that this distressing trend had appeared as early as the time of Tiberius (Tert. *De Pall.* 4.9; for a criticism of this passage see below): in AD 21 A. Caecina Severus (*PIR²* C 106; and *RE* Caecina [24]) reportedly petitioned the magistrates to enact legislation which would bring back the stola: see Scholz 1992: 17; McGinn 1998: 161–2. There is no extant law or *senatus consultum* concerning Caecina's petition. By AD 600, Isidore of Seville could write of the *stola* as a garment of the past (Isid. *Orig.* 19.25.3).

19. Scholz 1992: 33–74 for descriptions and notes; and (for instance) statues 8–14, 16, 19–21, 23, 25, 26, 28, 30 (Julio-Claudian); and 33–4 (Faustina Minor).

20. See for example Kleiner and Matheson 1996: 172, no. 126 (AD 98–117, Metropolitan Museum of Art, New York, Fletcher Fund, no. 1927, 12.122.4); of women in the eastern Empire, R. MacMullen 1980. "Women in Public in the Roman Empire." *Historia* 29: 217, n. 40. The paintings in the Praedium of Julia Felix at Pompeii show women in the Forum with unveiled heads (see S. Cirro Nappo. 1989. "Fregio dipinto dal <praedium> di Giulia Felice con rappresentazione del foro di Pompei." *Rivista di Studi Pompeiani* 3: 79–96, esp. figs 2, 3, 7).

    MacMullen (above, 217–18) states that veiling was less common among ladies of the upper classes than of the lower because of the strong influence of the Imperial family; which is not altogether tenable: in fact it appears (to judge from admittedly comparative evidence) that the lower-class women were much *less* likely to go about veiled, as the mantle was a hindrance to manual labor (see E. W. Fernea and R. A. Fernea. 1987. "Symbolizing Rules: Behind the Veil." In J. P. Spradley and D. W. McCurdy (eds), *Conformity and Conflict: Readings in Cultural Anthropology*, 6th edn, p. 106. Boston:

Little, Brown. M. M. Levine (1995. "The Gendered Grammar of Ancient Mediterranean Hair." In W. Doniger and H. Eilberg-Schwartz (eds), *Off With Her Head: The Denial of Women's Identity in Myth, Religion, and Culture*, pp. 76–130. Berkeley, CA: University of California Press) believes that veiling for lower-class women was "probably a reality" (p. 104); Propertius, however (2.23.13), implies that humbler women went unveiled (*reiecto . . . amictu*). On the other hand, the type of artistic record in which the *palla* is most in evidence is the funerary relief, a source which usually (though not always) depicts freedwomen and their families. For examples, see conveniently D. E. E. Kleiner. 1975. *Roman Group Portraiture: The Funerary Reliefs of the Late Republic and Early Empire*. New York: Garland Publishers. It is difficult to detect the *stola* in such reliefs, not because freedwomen were "barred" from wearing it, but probably because the *palla* was a much more visible and therefore significant sign of the ideal decorum, chastity, and social status of the Roman *matrona*: a set of behavioral characteristics that a freedwoman would be the more anxious to display, as they could indicate she was (as a freedwoman, not a slave) bound to her partner in a *iustum matrimonium*. See M. George, *Family Imagery and Family Values in Roman Italy*, Forthcoming.

21. I cannot locate an ancient reference indicating that Augustus also legislated the return of the *stola* and *vittae* along with the toga (*contra* Sebesta 1997: 531; and P. Zanker 1988: 165–6, see above, n. 17), although this might possibly be inferred from artistic evidence.

22. *Contra* L. Sensi, "Ornatus e status sociale delle donne romane," *ALFPer* no. 54 (1980–81): 60. S. E. Wood (1999. *Imperial Women: A Study in Public Images, 40 BC–AD 68*, p. 98. Leiden and Boston, MA: Brill), however, emphasizes the possibility that the *vittae* may have been painted into the braids of hair on statues—paint which has now of course disappeared. Compare the obvious fillets on a statue of Agrippina I (AD 23) on which the *vittae* are very clear: Inst. Neg. Rom. 61.1730 (see conveniently Scholz 1992: fig. 25); LaFollette 1995: fig. 3.6 (detail of the head of a Vestal Virgin from frieze B of the Cancellaria reliefs [late Flavian], now in the Lateran museum, Vatican). Some *vittae* were made of pearls or other precious stones rather than wool: *Dig.* 34.2.25.2 and 34.2.25.10.

23. Ovid *Ars* 1.31–32: *este procul, vittae tenues, insigne pudoris,/quaeque tegis medios, instita longa pedes*. See also Hor. *Sat.* 1.2.94–9; Tib. 1.6.67–8; Ovid *Pont.* 3.3.51. Prop. 4.11.61, in which a woman talks of having worn a matron's robe of honor (*et tamen emerui generosos vestis honores*), is clearly a reference to the *stola* and not, as the editor of the Loeb volume states, an allusion to a mysterious robe "earned by women who had borne three children" (p. 445). Such a garment is unknown in ancient literature. For a similar error, see W. A. Camps (ed.) 1965. *Propertius, Elegies Book IV*, p. 162. Cambridge: Cambridge University Press.

24. Mart. *Epig.* 10.5.1–2: *quisquis stolaeve purpuraeve contemptor/quos colere debet laesit impio versu* . . . See also Pliny *HN* 33.40; *ILLRP* 977 (on which see Palmer 1998: 30). Holtheide 1980 (above, n. 3) shows that the title of *matrona* or *femina stolata* arises in the third century and was applied to wives in a certain sector of the equestrian order (p. 130). To judge from artistic evidence, it appears that this phrase did not reflect sartorial reality but was merely employed as convenient legal shorthand.

25. On the clothing of prostitutes see now McGinn 1998: 156–71, 208–11 with exhaustive references and bibliography. Navigating the subject was made considerably easier by his scholarship. Gardner 1986: 129, 251–2 gives a briefer account. See also Dyck 2001: 127; and Heskel 1995: 140–1. On prostitution in antiquity, see further Adams 1983; Flemming 1999; H. Herter. 1960. "Die Soziologie der antiken Prostitution im Lichte des heidnischen und christlichen Schrifttums." *Jahrbuch für Antike und Christentum* 3: 70–111, and "Dirne," 1957. *Reallexikon für Antike und Christentum* III, pp. 1149–213. Stuttgart: Hiersemann; McGinn 1998; and B. Stumpp. 1998. *Prostitution in der römischen antike.* Berlin: Akademie.

26. Mart. *Epig.* 2.39: *vis dare quae meruit munera? mitte togam.* McGinn 1998: 163 interprets this passage as a joke: i.e., the gift of the toga anticipates her conviction under the existing statute. Courtney characterizes this epigram as "ambiguous" (Courtney 1980: 133 [at Juv. *Sat.* 2.68–70]).

27. Mart. *Epig.* 10.52: *Thelyn viderat in toga spadonem/damnatam Numa dixit esse moecham.* See McGinn 1998: 163.

28. Juv. *Sat.* 2.68–70: . . . *est moecha Fabulla,/damnetur, si vis, etiam Carfinia: talem/non sumet damnata togam.* Again, see McGinn 1998: 164.

29. Mart. *Epig.* 6.64.4: *sed patris ad speculum tonsi matrisque togatae.* Courtney 1980: 133 (at Juv. *Sat.* 2.68–70) again states that Martial's point is "ambiguous."

30. Hor. *Serm.* 1.2.63: *quid interest in matrona, ancilla peccesne togata?* The passage is perplexing. Most editors and translators (e.g., E. Fraenkel. 1957. *Horace,* p. 78, n. 2. Oxford: Oxford University Press and N. Rudd. 1966. *The Satires of Horace: A Study,* p. 11. Cambridge: Cambridge University Press) interpret the line as follows: if a man insists on ruining his reputation and squandering his fortune on a woman, what does it matter if he sins with a married woman or with a togate slave girl? But assuming *togata* is an adjective modifying *ancilla* is problematic: if a freedwoman turned prostitute, she would not be designated *ancilla.* She could be a slave girl kept as a togate prostitute, but the word *ancilla* in this case would be redundant, and the only time in the literature (as far as I am aware) that the two words occur together. An *ancilla* is ready with her sexual favors by virtue of being an *ancilla*; she does not need to be described

as togate. Instead, it makes more sense to take *togata* as a substantive, so that three categories of women are posited: married women, slave girls, and prostitutes/adulteresses, women to whom three separate categories of sexual conduct apply. Married women keep their charms hidden, and are dangerous; slave girls can be used sexually at virtually any time; *togatae* are very visible women and sleeping with them may involve an outlay of cash but no subterfuge. R. Bentley (1978 [1869]. *Q. Horatius Flaccus, Ex recensione et cum notis* vol. I, p. 352. New York: Garland Publishers) in fact interprets line 63 of this *Sermo* as referring to three separate types of women.

On the other side of the argument, many brothel workers are spoken of as slaves (though not as togate): Tarsia in the *Historia Apollonii Tyriensis* is sold as a slave to a brothel keeper (*Hist. Ap. Tyr.* 33–6, cit. K. R. Bradley. 1987. *Slaves and Masters in the Roman Empire: A Study in Social Control.* Oxford: Oxford University Press p. 117). In Apuleius' *Metamorphoses*, Charite is about to be enslaved to a brothel (*cum lupanari servierit*; Apul. *Met.* 7.9). In *Dig.* 3.2.4.2, one is called a pimp who has kept a brothel using free girls or slave girls: *ait praetor: "qui lenocinium fecerit." lenocinium facit qui quaestuaria mancipia habuerit: sed et qui in liberis hunc quaestum exercet, in eadem causa est.* Abandoned children were also sometimes brought up as prostitutes: see J. Boswell. 1988. *The Kindness of Strangers*, pp. 112–13. New York: Pantheon Books, with references. On prostitution and slavery, see Flemming 1999: 41, 56–61. Husband: Hor. *Serm.* 1.2.82: . . . *atque etiam melius persaepe togatae est.*

31. Porph. schol. Hor. sat. 1.2.63: *togatae autem in publicum procedere cogebantur feminae adulterii admissi convictae.*

32. Cic. *Phil.* 2.44: *sumpsisti virilem, quam statim muliebrem togam reddidisti. Primo vulgare scortum, certa flagitii merces, nec ea parva.* See Dyck 2001: 127.

33. [Tib.] 3.16.3–5: *sit tibi cura togae potior pressumque quasillo/ scortum quam Servi filia Sulpicia.* See Dalby 2000: 264.

34. Non. 653L: *dicitur et tectum* [sc. toga]. *Titinius Gemina* (p. 43): *"si rus cum scorto constituit ire, clavis ilico abstrudi iubeo rusticae togai nec sit copia," id est, tecti.* Elucidated by McGinn 1998: 158: "toga means both 'roof' and 'prostitute's garment' and then by synecdoche 'house (to have sex in)' and 'prostitute (to have sex with)'."

35. [Acro] schol. Hor. 1.2.63: *matronae, quae ob adulterium a maritis repudiabantur, togam accipiebant sublata stola propter ignominiam; toga autem meretrici apta. ita enim solebant prostare cum solis pullis togis, ut discernerentur a matronis; et ideo quae adulterii damnatae fuerant, hac veste utebantur. aliter: togatae dicebantur in publicum procedere feminae adulterii admissi <causa>. alii togatam dicunt libertinam, quia antea libertinae toga utebantur, stola vero matronae.* See McGinn 1998: 165–6, with references; certain portions of this text are also found in the third-century commentator Porphyrio; which text has *convictae* in place of *causa*.

36. The toga was, in fact, originally worn by both sexes, and it is unclear when and why the toga went from being the normal dress of a woman to the dress of a whore or adulteress. Non. 867–8L: "Not only men, but even women used to wear the toga. Afranius in his *Fratriae* (p. 182): 'Indeed, she was standing there eating lunch with us dressed in a toga.' Varro in Book I of his *De Vita Populi Romani*: '. . . once the toga was the common garment for both night and day, for both men and women'" (*Toga non solum viri sed etiam feminae utebantur, Afranius Fratriis* (p. 182): "*et quidem prandere stantem nobiscum, incinctam toga.*" *Varro de vita populi Romani lib. 1*: "*. . . praeterea quod in lecto togas ante habebant. ante enim olim toga fuit conmune vestimentum et diurnum et nocturnum et muliebre et virile*"). See also Serv. *ad Aen.* 1.282: ". . . both sexes and all social strata used to wear the toga" (*. . . et sexus omnis et condicio toga utebatur*). To confuse matters further, the toga was at some point in Rome's history a mark of status or honor for a woman (Pliny tells of the equestrian statue of the Republican heroine Cloelia, which was clad in a toga [510–509 BC; Pliny *HN* 34.28]; Dyck 2001: 127, n. 28 writes that "the toga for prostitutes is . . . a relic of the original unisex toga, from which the *stola* of the Roman matron was a departure," and does not take this passage into account. Furthermore, an article of male clothing called a "*stola*" (probably simply meaning "garment") does appear in one of Ennius' plays (Enn. *Telephus*, 339, 341), but whether this was a Roman garment or a Greek one is uncertain.

37. Contra McGinn 1998: 160. On Coan silk, see below, n. 67–70 .

38. See Adams 1983: 350–1. Flemming 1999: 57 states that usually the *matrona* is contrasted with the *moecha* in elegy and epigram, not with the *meretrix*, who "is again excluded from these elite literary conversations." But in terms of clothing, the terms of comparison do seem to be that of *matrona* and whore.

39. On which, see now McGinn 1998: 156–93; Gardner 1986: 127–32.

40. J. P. V. D. Balsdon. 1962. *Roman Women: Their History and Habits*, p. 252. London: Bodley Head; Courtney 1980: 133; McGinn 1998: 156, 166, 168. Gardner 1986: 251–2 discounts this, stating that the implication of Juvenal *Sat.* 2.68–70 is that convicted adulteresses did not have to wear the toga (but the phrase *talem . . . togam* surely implies a specific *type* of toga: namely, a transparent or gauzy one).

41. Prostitution was only punishable as a crime if the woman was of the upper classes: see McGinn 1998: 156–71. The supposition that prostitutes in antiquity were "compelled" to wear the toga raises other interesting questions, for which unfortunately the evidence is missing. Would the practitioner of only casual prostitution (on which see Flemming 1999: 42; and *Dig.* 23.2.43.2) have worn the toga? Would wearing the toga have been a humiliating mark of distinction (see Tacitus' *Germania* 19 in which an adulteress' hair is cropped short: *abscisis crinibus*), or a benefit, seeing that the prostitute might

attract more customers? As Gardner 1986: 252 remarks, "it would hardly seem necessary to compel prostitutes to adopt a style of dress different from other women." In fifteenth-century Venice, legislators decreed that whores would wear yellow scarves; in Milan white cloaks, later changed to black (Hughes 1983: 92). It is unclear how these vestimentary regulations were enforced. Communal officials in Genoa collected taxes from bordellos in the early fifteenth century, but there is no evidence that they also patrolled whores' clothing.

42. McGinn 1998: 166, n. 203 seems to link the dark-colored toga to the *colores meretricios* of Seneca (*NQ* 7.31.2); surely incorrect, as *pullus* was also the color of mourning (see Livy 45.7.4; Tac. *Hist.* 3.67; Flor. *Epit.* 2.13.45; Ovid does mention the color, however, as an attractive color for pale-skinned women [*Ars* 3.189], so the color was not strictly funereal). Although dark gray was sometimes associated with artisans and the poor (see Cic. *Ver.* 2.4.54, Calp. *Ecl.* 7.26–9; Mart. *Epig.* 10.76.8), white was not in any sense "restricted to" or "reserved for" the upper classes, except inasmuch as the color was probably hard to care for and expensive to keep clean. White as a clothing color for women is not in fact mentioned very often (at Ovid *Am.* 3.2.41; *Ars* 3.191–2; Hor. *Serm.* 1.2.36 [although the phrase is *cunni . . . albi*]). See André 1949: 25–42 on Latin terms for white, shades of color (and meaning), and references.

43. See McGinn 1998: 167: "the conclusion that not all Roman prostitutes wore the toga is supported by the wealth of evidence on the variety of garments worn by prostitutes."

44. Plaut. *Poen.* 191–2: *oculos volo meos delectare munditiis meretriciis;* Plaut. *Epid.* 222: *sed vestita, aurata, ornata, ut lepide, ut concinne, ut nove.* See also *Epid.* 214, in which the harlots are *ornatae.* Sen. *Controv.* 1.2.7: *stetisti sic ornata ut populo placere posses, ea veste quam leno dederat.* Sen. *NQ* 7.31.2: *colores meretricios matronis quidem non induendos viri sumimus.* Tac. *Dial.* 26: *adeo melius est orationem vel hirta toga induere quam fucatis et meretriciis vestibus insignire.*

45. Non. 868L: *apud veteres subcinctiore veste utebantur. Afranius* Excepto (p. 133): *"meretrix cum veste longa?"—"peregrino in loco solent tutandi causa sese sumere."* The fact that this quotation immediately follows Nonius' assertion that prostitutes wore a garment that was short may mean *veste longa* here merely refers to a long gown (*contra* McGinn 1998: 158 and A. Daviault. 1981. *Comoedia Togata: Fragments*, p. 180, n. 12. Paris: Belles Lettres). Juv. *Sat.* 8.158 notes that tavern-girl Cyane is *succincta* (wearing a tunic which has been tucked up into her belt, presumably exposing her legs). Tavern-girls were assumed by the Roman legal sources to be prostitutes: *Dig.* 23.2.43 pr. The over-dress of a *matrona* goes by various names in classical literature. The phrase *veste longa* is used by Ovid (*Fasti* 4.134) either specifically in reference to the *stola* or simply to indicate

the long gown of a respectable woman (see also Quint. *Instit.* 11.1.3., in which the phrase likely refers merely to a long gown and not specifically the *stola*). Tibullus refers to a *stola longa* at 1.6.68, as does Ovid at *Pont.* 3.3.52; Ovid uses the phrase *longa instita* at *Ars* 1.32 and *Trist.* 2.248. Long and concealing gowns seemed to be the ideal clothing of the respectable woman, and several authors complain that one therefore could not examine such women for physical flaws before taking them to bed: Mart. *Epig.* 11.104.7; Hor. *Serm.* 1.2.83–85, 96–100; Sen. *Frag. De Matr.* 50 (F. Haase (ed.) 1902. *L. Annaei Senecae opera quae supersunt.* Leipzig: Teubner).

46. Isid. *Orig.* 19.25.5: *amiculum est meretricum pallium lineum. hunc apud veteres matronae in adulterio deprehensae induebantur, ut in tali amiculo potius quam in stola polluerent pudicitiam. erat enim apud veteres hoc signum meretriciae vestis, nunc in Hispania honestatis.*

47. Ev. *Com.* 8.6. McGinn 1998: 159.

48. Xenophon, *Ephesiaca* 5.7. The slave collar of a *meretrix* from the Bulla Regia in Africa (*ILS* 9455) is a sobering example of prostitute adornment and one which "emphasizes the coercive element of prostitution" (Flemming 1999: 43 n. 21).

49. Juv. *Sat.* 3.66: *barbara mitra;* Juv. *Sat.* 6.120–4. Sedans: Juv. *Sat.* 3.135–6: *cum tibi vestiti facies scorti placet, haeres/et dubitas alta Chionen deducere sella.* On sedans and litters, see Adams 1983: 329–30; T. A. J. McGinn. 1998. "*Feminae probosae* and the litter." *Classical Journal* 93: 241–50. Hair dye/perfume: Prud. *Hamart.* 315 (*pigmentato . . . crine*).

50. Cat. 55.11–12: *quaedam inquit, nudum reduc<ta pectus>,/"en, hic in roseis latet papillis."*

51. See Ovid *Trist.* 2.309–10: *saepe supercilii nudas matrona severi/et veneris stantis ad genus omne videt.* Tac. *Ann.* 15.37; Petr. *Satyr.* 7; Juv. *Sat.* 6. 122; Juv. *Sat.* 11.171–3: *audiat ille/testarum crepitus cum verbis, nudum olido stans/fornice mancipium quibus abstinet, ille fruatur/vocibus obscaenis omnique libidinis arte . . .* (cf. Hor. *Serm.* 1.2.30 [*olenti in fornice stantem*]). Of course, for the Romans, nudity was also a sign of divinity (E. D'Ambra. 1996. "The Calculus of Venus: Nude Portraits of Roman Matrons." In N. Kampen (ed.), *Sexuality in Ancient Art*, pp. 219–32. Cambridge and New York: Cambridge University Press) and a "costume:" (L. Bonfante. 1989. "Nudity as a Costume in Classical Art." *American Journal of Archaeology* 93: 543–79). On dressed and nude female statues, see now three essays which have appeared in D. E. E. Kleiner and S. B. Matheson (eds) 2000. *I Claudia II.* Austin, TX: University of Texas Press: M. T. Boatwright. "Just Window Dressing?: Imperial Women as Architectural Sculpture" (pp. 61–76); S. B. Wood. "Mortals, Empresses, and Earth Goddesses: Demeter and Persephone in Public and Private Apotheosis" (pp. 77–100); and E. D'Ambra. "Nudity

and Adornment in Female Portrait Sculpture of the 2nd Century AD"
(pp. 101–14).

52. My thanks go to *Fashion Theory*'s anonymous referee for this point.
Cic . *Phil.* 3.12 and 13.31; on this see Heskel 1995: 137. Matrons
were supposed to be modestly well-covered: see Hor. *Serm.* 1.2.29.

53. The wall paintings in the brothel at Pompeii (VII, 12, 18–20) seem
to be an obvious place to look for artistic evidence concerning the
appearance of prostitutes (conveniently reproduced in J. Clarke.
1998. *Looking at Lovemaking: Constructions of Sexuality in Roman
Art 100 BC–AD 250*, figs. 83–5. Berkeley, CA: University of California
Press). But given the elaborate settings and rich bedcoverings present
in the paintings, and, in one (Clarke, fig. 83), the fancy hairdo of
the woman, it is dangerous to assume that these paintings are anything more than "upper-class fantasies for the lower-class viewer"
(Clarke, p. 202). In other words, it is unlikely that the pictures
represent the doings of the brothel girls (or even prostitutes) and their
clients, although Clarke tentatively suggests that perhaps the woman
in fig. 83 is meant to represent a high-class whore or *hetaira* (p. 202).
In one such fresco, in which the paint has survived to an extent that
it is possible to make any observations, the woman does appear to
be wearing the *strophium* (Clarke, fig. 84; cf. fig. 100). There exist
other wall paintings with erotic subjects in which female sexual
participants wear the *strophium* (see again Clarke, plates 7 and 8),
but there is nothing to suggest that these women are exclusively
prostitutes.

54. Plaut. *Miles* 790–3: *itaque eam huc ornatum adducas, ex matronarum
modo, capite compto, crinis vittasque habeat, adsimuletque se tuam
esse uxorem.* See also Serv. *ad Aen.* 7.403: *crinales vittas quae solarum
matronarum erant: nam meretricibus non dabantur;* Ovid *Fasti*
4.134; Mart. *Epig.* 1.35.8–9: *quis Floralia vestit et stolatum/permittet
meretricibus pudorem?* Unfortunately Martial gives no specific details
of prostitute garments.

55. *Dig.* 47.10.15.15: *si quis virgines appellasset si tamen ancillari veste
vestitas, minus peccare videtur: multo minus, si meretricia veste
feminae, non matrum familiarum vestitae fuissent. si igitur non
matronali habitu femina fuerit et quis eam appellavit vel ei comitem
abduxit, iniuriarum tenetur.*

56. A puzzling fragment of Atta (*Aquis Caldis*) concerns prostitute clothing: "when like prostitutes they whore their way through the streets
adorned like us" (Non. 193L: *Atta* Aquis Caldis (33): *"cum meretricie
nostro ornatu per vias lupantur"*). The meaning of this passage is,
however, not quite clear: we do not know if a citizen woman, a
prostitute, or a man is speaking; thus the garment the whores are
wearing is likewise obscure. See Gardner 1986: 252; McGinn 1998:
158–9; Daviault 1981 (above, n. 45): 255–6. See also Non. 868L. A
few passages also hint that the matron's *stola* was a form of protection

from unwanted advances: the *Digest* passage above, n. 55; Non. 868L; Val. Max. 2.1.5a, Tert. *De Pall.* 4.9.

57. McGinn 1998: 160 is incorrect I think in asserting that therefore young unmarried woman who were not prostitutes were expected to adopt the dress of *matronae* (or at least abstain from wearing the toga). There is no evidence that the *stola* was ever assumed by anyone other than a married woman—and, Tertullian claims (somewhat unbelievably), whores (*De Pall.* 4.9). Although we hear about none in the sources, unmarried women would surely have laid aside their childish toga at puberty (*contra* Sebesta 1995a: 50; this of course assumes girls wore the toga in the first place) and remain in the tunic, or the tunic and *palla*. McGinn 1998: 160, n. 163 is skeptical that the *toga praetexta* or purple-bordered toga was worn by girls but there is some literary evidence to support childish togas (Festus 282 L; Prop. 4.11.33; Arnobius, *Ad. Nat.* 2.67), as well as visual sources. For artistic examples of girls in the toga, see the collection in H. Gabelmann. 1985. "Römische Kinder in Toga Praetexta." *JDAI* 100: 517–27; H. R. Goette. 1990. *Studien zu römischen Togadarstellungen.* Mainz am Rhein: P. v. Zabern: especially plate 70, nos. 1 (girl in a toga, 50 BC, Musei Capitolini, Rome, no. 2176) and 5 (tombstone of Hateria Superba, Florence, Uffizi no. 1914.942); and Figure 1. If both children and whores *were* in the habit of wearing the toga, surely the broad purple stripe on the (well-born) girl's toga would have distinguished her from the prostitute.

58. There are too many instances in the sources of cosmetics on respectable women to enumerate here, but see for example Pliny *HN* 11.154; Cic. *Orat.* 78–9, Sen. *Controv.* 6.8; Juv. *Sat.* 6.477. For make-up on prostitutes, see Sen. *Consol. ad Helv.* 16.3. On ancient make-up, see now Richlin 1995 and Wyke 1994; as well as Kleiner and Matheson 1996: 160–1, 165, 175.

59. Thus, American aristocratic women utilized cosmetics, but the adjective "painted" was associated with whores (K. Peiss. 1990. "Making Faces: The Cosmetics Industry and the Cultural Construction of Gender 1890–1930." *Gender* 7: 143–6). L. Allason-Jones (1989. *Women in Roman Britain*, p. 130. London: British Museum Publications) feels it is difficult to judge whether women of the middling and lower classes used cosmetics, but according to other scholars, because of the status of beauty and the influence it gave women at all levels of society, "the use and prestige of cosmetics crossed economic boundaries." A woman did not need to be wealthy to wear perfumes or cosmetics: some inexpensive *pyxides* were made of wood, the blown glass used to hold unguents was cheap, and most substances used for cosmetics and scents (or substitutes for them) were widely available (see Kleiner and Matheson 1996: 164, and no. 118).

60. Sen. *Consol. ad Helv.* 16.3: *non te . . . periculosa etiam probis peiorum detorsit imitatio. Contra* S. Romm (1992. *The Changing*

Face of Beauty, p. 25. St. Louis, MI: Mosby), beauty ideals were not set solely by the artistically and socially powerful. The assertion that rich or royal women are the only ones who set trends because they are the only ones who can afford to have their portrait done ignores the fact that fashion can be influenced from below as well as from above (see A. Bonanno. 1988. "Imperial and Private Portraiture: A Case of Non-dependence." In N. Binacasa, and G. Rizza (eds), *Ritratto Ufficiale e Ritratto Privato. Atti della II Conferenza Internazionale sul Ritratto Romano*, pp. 157–64. Rome: Consiglio Nazionale delle Ricerche). In nineteenth-century America, because actresses or prostitutes set fashion, "if a woman wanted to look fashionable, she also ran the risk of looking immodest;" although famous courtesans were among the leaders of fashion, an elite woman could not follow their styles too closely (V. Steele. 1983. *Fashion and Eroticism*, p. 130. Oxford: Oxford University Press).

61. On the colors of Roman fabrics, see André 1949; R. J. Forbes. 1964. "Dyes and Dyeing," *Studies in Ancient Technology*, vol. IV, pp. 99–150. Leiden: Brill; Sebesta 1995b; and Wilson 1938: 6–13.

62. Plaut. *Epid.* 229–35; see Sebesta 1995b: 65. The alliteration present in this list of color terms is possibly due to Epidicus' desire to pull the wool over his master's eyes (see Wilson 1938: 154) as well as (to the male gaze?) the monolithic nature of all types of female adornment. It is important to note, however, that not all these color types are accepted translations of the word in question. *Caesicius* (which the *TLL* names as a word of uncertain etymology and meaning) occurs here and in Nonius (866L), and is often translated as "sky-blue" (perhaps from *caesius,* although *caesicius* does not appear in André 1949). *Caltula* is often translated simply as "a short undergarment" without reference to its distinctive color (see the *Oxford Latin Dictionary,* on the basis of Varr. *Gram.* 194 in Non. 880L, and Isid. *Orig.* 19.33.4), without giving details of its color, but Nonius names the *caltula* as a yellow garment, from *calta* (marigold), in conjunction with *crocotula* (from *croceus*; cf. *crocota*). On the derivation of *caltulus,* see also *Gloss. Plac.* 5.16.2 (52.5); Var. *L.* 5.131; Ps. Fulg. Rusp. *Serm.* 69, p. 942A; André 1949, 296; and T. E. Tucker. 1931. *A Concise Etymological Dictionary of Latin*, p. 42. Halle: Maxz Niemeyer. *Crocotulus* is one of a number of adjectives derived from, ultimately, *crocus* or *crocum* (see also *croceus* and *crocinus*; Plautus mentions *infectores corcotarii* at *Aul.* 521). See Non. 880L and André 1949: 153–5 for references and nuances of hue. *Cumatilis*: see also Non. 879L; Titin. *Com.* 114; Comm. *instr.* 1.10.3; André 1949: 193–4; Tucker 1931: 72 (above) states that it: "apparently <a *cumatos,* <κῦμα (wave)." *Carinus* or *caryinus* (from the Greek) is not found in André, it may in fact be the color of walnuts (see Pliny *HN* 15.28, 23.88), or it may be a variation of *cerinus* (also from the Greek; ancient wax was a pale yellow or [by refining] even white,

although it could also be colored artificially: see André 1949: 157–8, 296, 301; Non. 880L, Pliny *HN* 19.65, 37.47, 37.77). Cf. *cereus*: Calp. *Ecl.* 2.91; Mart. *Epig.* 1.92.7. My thanks to *Fashion Theory*'s anonymous referee here.

63. Ovid *Ars* 3.169–92; see Sebesta 1995b: 65. Again, the translation of these poetic descriptions into specific color terms is also one that is open to some interpretation. *Aer, aerius* and *aerinus* are not generally used in classical literature to indicate color (see André 1949: 182–3), and this instance in Ovid is, as André points out, poetic paraphrase. This is also true of *unda. Aureus* is of course a well-documented color term meaning bright yellow or gold (see complete references in the *TLL* [esp. 1491] and André 1949: 155–6 for the many different shades of this color; cf. *auratus* [André 1949: 156–7]). Although Ovid likely means simply yellow cloth in this instance, it could also be the case that the cloth was interwoven with golden threads or ornaments (see André 1949: 155; Sebesta 1995b: 66, 68, 70, 71 for references to golden cloth). *Paphiae myrti*, another instance of poetic description, likely represent a similar color to *myrteus*, either dark green like the leaves or brown like the bark (see Petr. *Satyr.* 21.2; Tib. 3.4.28, for instance; and André 1949: 190–1 for complete references). *Purpurae amethysti* is likely meant to be the color *amethystinus* (violet-blue; see André 1949: 196–7). Pliny the Elder uses this term somewhat interchangeably with *ianthinus* and *violaceus. Albentes rosae* is a phrase usually translated as pale pink, but is a difficult color to identify, as *albens* denotes a very light gray (Sebesta 1995b: 68), but can also mean simply pale (for *roseus*, see André 1949: 111–12). *Glandes* and *amygdala* are both technically nuts: acorns a dark brown color with red undertones, and almonds a light beige (see Sebesta 1995b: 68. André 1949 does not name either; but see pp. 123–5 on *fuscus*). For *pullus*, see above, n. 42.

64. Apul. *Met.* 7.8. See also Livy 34.1.3; Apul. *Met.* 8.27; Petr. *Satyr.* 131. For white as a color for women, see above, n. 42.

65. Plautus wrote that a purple makes a pretty girl seem overdressed (*nimis ornata est*; *Most.* 290). But Caesar's restrictions on purple (Suet. *Iul.* 43) assumes women wore the color often, and Ovid begs women not to wear purple continually (*Ars* 3.169–72). See also Non. 862L for an entirely purple *stola*; and Val. Max. 5.2.1a. For purple generally, see M. Reinhold. 1970. *The History of Purple as a Status Symbol in Antiquity*, p. 116. Brussels: Latomus; André 1949: 90–105, 195–9.

66. See Sebesta 1995b: 70–1, with notes. Petr. *Satyr.* 67. M. S. Smith (ed.) 1975. *Cena Trimalchionis*, pp. 54–8. Oxford: Oxford University Press asserts that "there is a notable frequency of red and green in the description of Trimalchio and his surroundings," but believes these colors were chosen merely for their sharp contrast; he does not point out they might be indicative of social status. But Smith does

suggest (p. 187) that perhaps *galbinus* (a bright greenish yellow) was an unsuitable color to be worn by a man because it denoted effeminacy (see Juv. *Sat.* 2.97; Mart. *Epig.* 1.96.9). *Prasinus, venetus,* and *russeus* were also colors of the charioteers (or their factions) in the Circus (see Sebesta 1995b: 70 and references to André 1949 following). *Prasinus:* Suet. *Calig.* 55.2, *Nero* 22.1; *CIL* 6.10047; Petr. *Satyr.* 70; Mart. *Epig.* 10.48.23, 11.33.1; André 1949: 192. *Venetus:* Suet. *Vit.* 7.1, 14.3, *CIL* 6.10047.a.3, 6.37835; Mart. *Epig.* 6.46.1, 14.131.1; André 1949: 181–2. *Russatus:* Juv. *Sat.* 7.114; *CIL* 6.10048.1, 14.2884; *russeus:* André 1949: 83–4. See also T. J. Leary. 1996. *Martial Book XIV: The Apophoreta,* pp. 195–6. London: Duckworth. Photis: Apul. *Met.* 2.7. Dinner dress: Mart. *Epig.* 10.29.4. See also the green fan at Mart. *Epig.* 3.82.1 (used by a concubine to fan Zoilus, a host of many vices, including miserliness and effeminacy).

67. Sen. *Consol. ad Helv.* 16.4: *numquam tibi placuit vestis, quae nihil amplius nudaret, cum poneretur.* Pliny the Elder gives credit for the invention of Coan silk to a woman named Pamphile, daughter of Plateas, "who has the undeniable distinction of having devised a plan to reduce women's clothing to nakedness" (*HN* 11.76: *prima eas redordiri rursusque texere invenit in Coo mulier Pamphile, Plateae filia, non fraudanda gloria excogitatae rationis ut denudet feminas vestis*).

68. Sen. *De Benef.* 7.9.5: *video sericas vestes, si vestes vocandae sunt, in quibus nihil est, quo defendi aut corpus aut denique pudor possit, quibus sumptis parum liquido nudam se non esse iurabit.*

69. Prop. 1.2.2, 2.1.5–6, 4.2.23; Hor. *Serm.* 1.2.101–2: *Cois tibi paene videre est/ut nudam . . .* Coan silk was doubly dangerous, because it was expensive and could therefore could display female power and status (see Tib. 2.4.29, in which it is classed with other expensive gifts such as Tyrian purple and pearls; and Coan silk could also be striped with gold, *illa gerat vestes tenues, quas femina Coa/texuit, auratas disposuitque vias* [Tib. *ibid*].).

70. Modern scholars have concluded that Coan silk was in fact *tusseh* or 'wild' silk. On ancient silk, see F. E. Day. 1956. "Aristotle: *Ta bombukia.*" In *Studi Orientalistici in onore di Giorgio Levi della Vida,* vol. I, pp. 207–18. Rome: Instituto per l'oriente; and W. T. M. Forbes. 1930. "The Silkworm of Aristotle." *Classical Philology* 25: 22–6. See also Forbes 1964 (above, n. 61): 49–58. On the differences between wild silk and Chinese silk, see Dalby 2000: 151–152.

71. Juv. *Sat.* 6. 589–91; Pliny the Elder, *HN* 33.152 (see also *HN* 33.40, in which Pliny complains of women of equestrian families wearing gold. Pearls: Pliny *HN* 9.114. For costume pearls, see below, n. 72.

72. Emeralds: Isid. *Orig.* 16.15.27. Opals: Pliny *HN* 37.83. Carbuncles and topazes: Pliny *HN* 37.112. Sapphires: Pliny *HN* 36.198. See M. L. Trowbridge. 1930. *Philological Studies in Ancient Glass.*

University of Illinois Studies in Language and Literature 13 (Urbana, IL): 144–50 for further examples and exhaustive references. Pearls could be replicated "by thinly coating an alabaster bead with silver" (see Kleiner and Matheson 1996: 175), but Trowbridge postulates that pearls could also be imitated in glass (p. 147; see Tert. *Ad Mart.* 4; Hier. *Epist.* 29.7.8 and 130.6.6). At Petr. *Satyr.* 67, Scintilla's earring is called "a glass bean" (*faba vitrea*).

73. *Cod. Theodos.* 15.7.11; In the fifteenth century, Siena allowed its prostitutes platform shoes, embroidered fabrics, and cloth of gold in an effort to weaken the appeal of finery for respectable women (Hughes 1983: 92).

74. Sen. *Controv.* 2.7.4. Tertullian: on this passage, see McGinn 1998: 161, and C. Tibiletti. 1981. "La donna in Tertulliana." In *Misoginia e maschilismo in Grecia e Roma. Pubblicazioni dell'Istituto di filologia classica e medievale* 71, pp. 69–85. Genova: Istituto di filologia classica e medievale. On women's clothing, see L. Raditsa. 1985. "The Appearance of Women and Contact: Tertullian's *De Habitu Feminarum*." *Athenaeum* 73: 297–326.

75. Tert. *De Pall.* 4.9; *De Cult. Fem.* 2.12.3 (*quid non meos mores habitus praenuntiat*) and 2.12.2: *quas si quae leges a maritalibus et matronalibus decoramentis coercebant, iam certe saeculi improbitas quotidie insurgens honestissimis quibusque feminis usque ad errorem dignoscendi coaequavit?* The *leges* are unspecified.

76. Sen. *Controv.* 2.7.9: *feminae quidem unum pudicitia decus est; itaque ei curandum est esse ac videri pudicam.*

77. Sen. *Controv.* 2.7.4: *cum tot argumentis inpudicitiam praescripseritis, cultu, incessu, sermone, facie.*

78. Sen. *Controv.* 2.7.3: *matrona, quae <tuta> esse adversus sollicitatoris lasciviam volet, prodeat in tantum ornata quantum ne inmunda sit.* On *cultus* as status, see D'Ambra 1996 and D'Ambra 2000 (both above, n. 51).

79. Juvenal however gives two instances in which women become aroused by watching an overtly sexual theatrical display: Juv. *Sat.* 6.63–66 and 11.168–70.

80. Prop. 3.21.3: *crescit enim assidue spectando cura puellae* (see also Ovid *Am.* 2.19.19); Ovid *Am.* 2.2.3–4, 3.2.34; Tert. *De Spect.* 25.

81. Ovid *Ars* 1.99–100: *spectatum veniunt, veniunt spectentur ut ipsae:/ ille locus casti damna pudoris habet.* See also Plaut. *Poen.* 337; Aelian *Var. Hist.* 7.10; Juv. *Sat.* 3.65 mentions prostitutes ordered (presumably by their pimps/owners) to display themselves at the Circus (*ad circum iussas prostare*).

82. Sen. *Controv.* 1.2.5: *meretrix vocata es, in communi loco stetisti, superpositus est cellae tuae titulus, venientem recepisti.* The whore is also described as "wheedling" in *Controv.* 1.2.2 (*blanda est;* see also Ovid *Am.* 1.15.18), 1.2.5 (*docetur blanditias*), 1.2.12 (*blanda sit*). Seneca does not say whether she was naked or clothed; this

particular girl was displayed for sale naked (1.2.3), but this was before she was taken to the brothel. *Blanditia* (flattery, coaxing) is often employed in the sources by men or women to secure erotic advantage: at Mart. 12.97.8, a rich wife tries to coax an erection from her husband (who prefers boys) *vocibus blandis* (and see Ovid *Am.* 3.7 *passim*); at *Am.* 2.1.21 Ovid uses *blanditia* in an attempt to open his beloved's door; at 3.2.55 Venus herself is described as *blanda*. The *Digest* defines *appellare* as *oratio blanda*: "to accost is to make an attempt upon another's virtue with smooth words; this is not shouting but an attempt contrary to sound morals" (*Dig.* 47.10.15.20: *appellare est blanda oratione alterius pudicitiam adtemptare: hoc enim non est convicium, sed adversus bonos mores adtemptare*). In Juv. *Sat.* 11.171–4, an uncouth man uses language so foul even a naked whore would not employ it (presumably with her customers; see above, n. 51). Whores were notoriously shameless: Ovid *Met.* 10.238–242 the "first" prostitutes (the *obscenae Propoetides*) become so hardened that their shame vanishes (*pudor cessit*) and they lose the power to blush (*sanguisque induruit oris*). Cf. *Anth. Pal.* 5.46 [Philodemus 4].

83. Sen. *Controv.* 1.2.5: *in omnem corporis motum confingitur.*

84. One word for a whore in Latin was *circulatrix*, "she who walks;" (e.g., *Priap.* 19.1); in other words, a whore who paraded through the streets displaying her body to potential customers (see Adams 1983: 332).

85. Adams 1983: 335 explains *mulier secutuleia* (a "follow-me girl") at Petr. *Satyr.* 81.5 not as a prostitute but as a woman so desperate for intercourse she will pay for it (see also Juv. *Sat.* 10.319). Did only low women or prostitutes stand alone in the streets? See Adams 1983: 337 and Plaut. *Cist.* 331 (in which a *meretrix* exclaims that if she stands alone in the street she might be taken for a *prostibulum*, a low whore; a joke?).

References

Adams, J. N. 1983. "Words for 'prostitute' in Latin. *Rheinisches Museum* 126: 321–58.

André, J. 1949. "*Étude sur les termes de couleur dans la langue latine.*" Paris: Librairie C. Klincksieck.

Bradley, K. R. 1994. *Slavery and Society at Rome.* Cambridge, UK and New York: Cambridge University Press.

Brunt, P. A. 1988. *The Fall of the Roman Republic and Related Essays.* Oxford: Clarendon Press and Oxford, Toronto: Oxford University Press.

Courtney, E. 1980. *A Commentary on the Satires of Juvenal.* London: Athlone Press.

Dalby, A. 2000. *Empire of Pleasures: Luxury and Indulgence in the Roman World*. New York: Routledge.

Dyck, A. R. 2001. "Dressing to Kill: Attire as a Proof and Means of Characterization in Cicero's Speeches." *Arethusa* 34: 119–30.

Flemming, R. 1999. "*Quae corpore quaestum fecit*: The Sexual Economy of Female Prostitution in the Roman Empire." *Journal of Roman Studies* 89: 38–61.

Gardner, J. F. 1986. *Women in Roman Law and Roman Society*. Beckenham, Kent: Croom Helm.

Garnsey, P., and R. Saller. 1987. *The Roman Empire: Economy, Society, and Culture*. London: Duckworth.

Heskel, J. 1995. "Cicero as Evidence for Attitudes to Dress in the late Republic." In Sebesta and Bonfante 1995, pp. 133–45.

Hughes, D. Owen. 1983. "Sumptuary Law and Social Relations in Renaissance Italy." In J. Bossy (ed.), *Disputes and Settlements: Law and Human Relations in the West*, pp. 69–99. Cambridge and New York: Cambridge University Press.

Kleiner, D. E. E., and S. B. Matheson (eds) 1996. *I Claudia: Women in Ancient Rome*. New Haven, CT: Yale University Art Gallery; Austin, Tx: distributed by University of Texas Press.

LaFollette, L. 1995. "The Costume of the Roman Bride." In Sebesta and Bonfante 1995, pp. 54–64.

McGinn, T. A. 1998. *Prostitution, Sexuality, and the Law in Ancient Rome*. New York: Oxford University Press.

Palmer, R. E. A. 1998. *Bullae insignia ingenuitatis. American Journal of Ancient History* 14: 1–69.

Perrot, Philippe. 1994. *Fashioning the Bourgeoisie: A History of Clothing in the Nineteenth Century*. Trans. R. Bienvenu. Princeton, NJ: Princeton University Press.

Reinhold, M. 1971. "The Usurpation of Status and Status Symbols in the Roman Empire." *Historia* 20: 275–302.

Richlin, A. 1995. "Making up a Woman: The Face of Roman Gender." In W. Doniger and H. Eilberg-Schwartz (eds), *Off With Her Head: The Denial of Women's Identity in Myth, Religion, and Culture*, pp. 185–213. Berkeley, CA: University of California Press.

Scholz, B. 1992. *Untersuchungen zur Tracht der römischen matrona*. Köln: Böhlau.

Sebesta, J. L. 1995a. "Symbolism in the costume of the Roman Woman." In Sebesta and Bonfante 1995, pp. 46–53.

Sebesta, J. L. 1995b. "*Tunica ralla, tunica spissa*: The Colours and Textiles of Roman Costume." In Sebesta and Bonfante 1995, pp. 65–76.

Sebesta, J. L. 1997. "Women's costume and feminine civic morality in Augustan Rome." *Gender and History* 9.3: 529–41.

Sebesta, J. L., and L. Bonfante (eds) 1995. *The World of Roman Costume*. Madison, WI: University of Wisconsin Press.

Stone, S. 1995. "The Toga: From National to Ceremonial Costume." In Sebesta and Bonfante 1995, pp. 13–45.

Wilson, L. M. 1938. *The Clothing of the Ancient Romans.* Baltimore, MD: Johns Hopkins Press.

Wyke, M. 1994. "Woman in the Mirror: The Rhetoric of Adornment in the Roman World." In L. Archer *et al.* (eds), *Women in Ancient Societies: An Illusion of the Night,* New York: Routledge, pp. 134–51.

Fashion Theory, Volume 6, Issue 4, pp. 421–440
Reprints available directly from the Publishers.
Photocopying permitted by licence only.
© 2002 Berg. Printed in the United Kingdom.

Just a Fashion?: Cultural Cross-dressing and the Dynamics of Cross-cultural Representations

Inge Boer

Inge Boer is an Associate
Professor at the Institute for
Literary Studies, University of
Amsterdam, The Netherlands.
Her research and publications
focus on Orientalism in French
and British texts and imagery,
gender and (post-)colonial
discourse, cross-cultural
representations, and cultural
cross-dressing. Her book
*Disorienting Vision: Rereading
Stereotypes in French Orientalist
Texts and Images* is forthcoming.

Just a fashion? Why then debate the Rudolf Valentino lookalike turned female fortune-teller selling Diesel Jeans shorts through the message of love? (Figure 1). Just a fashion? Nothing to worry about, this modern woman (Figure 2) reclining on fur. Fashion tells us, as in *Belle de jour*, that we can safely mix different elements of the glamorous clothing of the 1996–97 Winter fashion. As the caption on the image states:

Sleek, ankle-length skirts and dresses, tantalizing slits and shiny ornaments. The attitude of Yves Saint-Laurent's muse Catherine Deneuve mixed with Bianca Jagger's and Jerry Hall's glamrock. Gold is OK, fake fur is chic and lurex no longer a superfluous luxury.

Figure 1

"The Secrets of Love." Diesel advertisement. In *Elle* (Dutch edn), March 1996. Permission by Diesel S. P. A. and by *Elle*.

The images, however, propose more than the latest in fashion and merit closer analysis. *Belle de jour*, Luis Buñuel's well-known film starring Catherine Deneuve, is only one of the possible connotations suggested by the title and text accompanying the photo. Other references are at play as well, such as those referring to the beauty of the woman in the photo as in "belle comme le jour" meaning "to be a divine beauty." Belle de jour also has a specific botanical meaning. Bindweed, a group of plants characterized by their twining and vine-like branches and stems, has flowers that are in bloom for one day only. Like the sinuous lines of a

Figure 2

"Belle de Jour." In *Elle* (Dutch edn), September 1996. Photo by permission of Cornelie Tollens (styling Marije Goekoop, make-up Eva Kapper) and by permission *Elle*.

twining plant, whose flowers quickly fade, the model's undulating form refers to a body, twisting and turning, displaying the precious beauty, distant and mysterious, of a Catherine Deneuve or, in the more outgoing version, of Bianca Jagger or Jerry Hall.

Drawing attention to the sinuous lines of the model's body, I want to point out the resemblance with the ways odalisques were depicted in Orientalist painting (Boer forthcoming), symbolized by the serpentine line and the eroticism of Jean-Dominique Ingres' *La grande odalisque* (Ockman 1995). Dressing as the Belle de jour, then, entices us into the world of movie stars and fashion models, both muses to stimulate men's inspiration, in which references—highly cultured—to the Orient are freely mixed with nature. An example for Western women? Just a fashion? It is not what you are, but what you want to be; moreover, it is not what you want to be, but what you want to become, temporarily, ambivalently, fictionally.

In the *Diesel* advertisement, a Diesel Magic Ball will tell you everything about the number 1 mystery for mankind since the Big Bang—that is, the secrets of love. Our Rudolf Valentino lookalike, whose very name is synonymous with love and who would send women swooning in days gone by, has been able to conjure up an image in his crystal ball: a young white woman is playing the innocent, yet her hands hold on to dangling strings of white beads or pearls which might surround her uncovered belly anytime to send her into the gyrations of a belly dancer. And what is this Orientalized gender-bender, cross-dressing as a woman, and yet maintaining his two-day beard, asking us to see? Why this mixing of Westernness and Orientalness? This simultaneous allusion to buying jeans and to fortune-tellers who cannot be assigned to one gender or to one cultural identity indicates the problems and complexities of cultural cross-dressing. Cultural cross-dressing refers to an *as if* situation. The fortune-teller dresses *as if* he were a woman, *as if* he were Oriental, the *Belle de jour* dresses in the latest fashion produced in the fashion capitals of the world, that still happen to be in Milan, Paris, London, and New York, and poses *as if* Oriental.

The term "cultural cross-dressing," then, conveys a sense of transgressing the boundaries not only in gender roles but also in cultural roles. Moreover, by using the term cultural cross-dressing I want to stress the fact that here, in the examples I analyze, it is directed toward the assumption of a culturally constructed model, i.e. the Orient. Cross-dressing also implies an act in which one consciously and for a period of time takes up a particular form of dress (see Boer 1994, 1998).

Fashion, as a highly developed system, functions in a capitalist world economy and proves to be an example *par excellence* of globalized production and consumption. Economy driven as it is, the fashion system poses questions of identity formation and cross-cultural representation. I deliberately call it a "fashion system," a sign system that can be analyzed semiotically in the ways it displays relations to class, gender, and ethnicity

(Barthes 1967). What makes cultural cross-dressing relevant is the pertinence of questions about inequalities of power. Who speaks for whom? What modes of cultural cross-dressing are preferred over others?

In fashion today, those questions are urgent, yet not foregrounded. Of course, fashion houses dictate trends, and even trends such as "anything goes;" designers decide about colors and fabrics, we may scream and rebel against the modern day despots of fashion but enough willing victims of the craze for Gucci shoes one year and Comme des Garçons suits another, keep the cheap labor in the free-trade zones of South-East Asia going, and the laws of fashion in place.[1] To give an example: the top Belgian designer Dries van Noten, who is known for his love of fabrics, and saris in particular, draws his inspiration from different parts of the globe: India is his muse one year, Africa the next, and Istanbul the year after. But in an interview he declared that he is interested "not [in] the purely Indian or African, but [in] the mixing of ingredients." He does not want to produce clients who are "living illustrations" or clones of the designer, instead he states: "I sell options to people, no lifestyle" (van der Haak 1996: 14).

Mixing ingredients and selling options may sound like the liberal message of the United Colors of Benetton: an unproblematic joining together of separate elements, temporarily grafting one piece of clothing onto another (Apter 1999: 19). Yet, this hybrid form is a far cry from the hybridity Homi Bhabha argues for, in which it becomes "an active moment of challenge and resistance against the dominant cultural power" (Bhabha paraphrased in Young 1995: 23). In *Colonial Desire* Robert Young traces the genealogy of hybridity, insisting that

> Hybridity . . . shows the connections between the racial categories of the past and contemporary cultural discourse: it may be used in different ways, given different inflections and apparently discrete references, but it always reiterates and reinforces the dynamics of the same conflictual economy whose tensions and divisions it re-enacts in its own antithetical structure (1995: 27).

Therefore, it is important to perceive cultural cross-dressing, as an instance making use of hybridity, in the tensions it evokes and the ambiguity it implies. A short detour will show how and why cultural cross-dressing needs to be contextualized historically.

Turqueries and Masquerades

I will focus on some early examples of cultural cross-dressing, and demonstrate the relevance of this theoretical term in the analysis of mid-eighteenth-century paintings of women, upper-class women, dressing up *as if* Oriental. All belong to the genre of the so-called turqueries, paintings

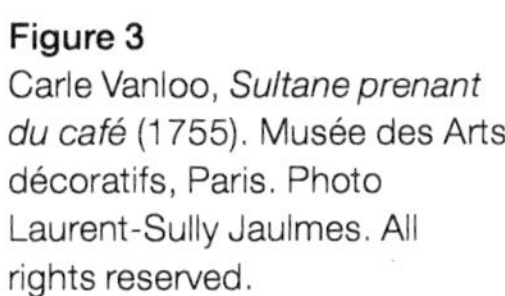

Figure 3
Carle Vanloo, *Sultane prenant du café* (1755). Musée des Arts décoratifs, Paris. Photo Laurent-Sully Jaulmes. All rights reserved.

of a fantasized Orient. The first two are by Carle Vanloo: *Sultane prenant du café* (1755) (Figure 3) and *Deux sultanes travaillant à la tapisserie* (1755) (Figure 4). The third is by Jean-Marc Nattier, *Sultane sortant du bain, servie par des esclaves* (1742) (Figure 5). All three paintings give ample reason to suppose that they are about the Orient—see for instance all the Oriental details—and therefore depict women in the Orient.

Figure 4
Carle Vanloo, *Deux sultanes travaillant à la tapisserie* (1755). Musée des Arts décoratifs, Paris. Photo Laurent-Sully Jaulmes. All rights reserved.

Figure 5
Jean-Marc Nattier, *Sultane
sortant du bain, servie par des
esclaves* (1742). Reproduced
by permission of the Trustees
of the Wallace Collection,
London. Visit the
Wallace Collection at
www.wallace-collection.org.uk

The genesis of turqueries has often been explained by historical factors. The visit by an Ottoman ambassador, Said Pasha, to Paris in 1742 functions in those explanations as the departure point for a true fashion craze to have oneself painted in Oriental dress.[2] This visit might have been a catalyst in promoting a fascination with otherness, but I would add that the contemporary media were instrumental in distributing accounts of Said Pasha's visit, his entourage, and the presents he brought with him. Pierre Martino (1906: 97–103) mentions issues of the *Mercure* entirely devoted to that visit and little pamphlets being published to keep the Parisian population up to date. However, the linear, deterministic relation between an event such as an embassy visit and a structural phenomenon such as the rapid proliferation of pictorial representations of women dressed as Oriental women is not satisfactory.

The reason for my dissatisfaction can be described in terms of the relation between text and context. In the interpretation mentioned above, the context functions as a given and determines the meaning of the event, thus establishing a one-to-one relation. Jonathan Culler (1988: ix) has pointed out that interpretive strategies determine a certain context. Context is produced and needs to be clarified as much as events (see also

Bryson 1994). Culler's apt term "framing" gives us a better grasp of the activity of contextualization and the agency involved. Therefore, instead of analyzing cultural cross-dressing as a static phenomenon, I want to elaborate on the ways it operates in a system of exchange, as a dynamic process. My framing centers on fashion, cross-dressing, and the shifts in roles they imply.

The phenomenon of an Oriental fashion could only operate, as Daniel Roche points out for fashion in general in *La culture des apparences* (1989), in a system of exchange where after the mid-eighteenth century a rapidly growing number of publications on clothing, costume, and what came to be called fashion developed. Cultural cross-dressing, therefore, is firmly embedded in relations of production and trade, of circulation of imagery and of, to use Roche's term, "a culture of appearances." In this culture of appearances, dress was a way to distinguish and to distinguish oneself; in short, dress can be interpreted as a sign system.[3] Colors, fabrics and ornaments functioned as signs to indicate and maintain social relations. With the advent of fashion conventional codes of dress became modified, but also installed the fear of confusion of class indicators and social values.

The notion of cross-dressing appeals to the fear of confusing categories as well as to the desire to distinguish (oneself). As the dictionary indicates, to transvest means to clothe across, i.e., in violation of custom. In their well-known study *The Tradition of Female Transvestism in Early Modern Europe* (1989), Rudolf Dekker and Lotte van de Pol indicate how female cross-dressers were seen as disturbing the existing arrangements between the sexes. Women dressing as men tried to escape the limitations that society imposed on them. All the women that Dekker and Van de Pol studied were lower-class women, who, according to contemporary court trial reports, by dressing as men "dressed *up*"—that is, they tried under false pretense to pose socially "higher," as men with all the advantages of masculine roles.

When we look at the examples of cultural cross-dressing, Dekker and Van de Pol's study raises some questions. How to interpret the issue of class as the women posing in the paintings under scrutiny here were upper-class women? If dressing as a man is considered "dressing *up*," how is cultural cross-dressing to be interpreted? Cross-dressing has also been analyzed in the context of the carnivalesque (Russo 1986) and the masquerade.

Cultural cross-dressing, however, differs in some important respects from masquerade. As Terry Castle analyzed in her book *Masquerade and Civilization* (1992), the masquerade, in its English eighteenth-century context, developed rapidly at the beginning of that century into a very popular and heavily criticized phenomenon. She states that:

> The masked assemblies of the eighteenth century were in the deepest sense a kind of collective meditation on self and other, and an exploration of their mysterious dialectic . . . The pleasure of the

masquerade attended on the experience of doubleness, the alien-
ation of inner from outer, a fantasy of two bodies simultaneously
and thrillingly present, self and other together, the two-in-one
(Castle 1992: 4–5).

Castle's emphasis is on the notion of self, which, in masquerading, remained
elusive and inaccessible as a way to devalue unitary notions of the self
in ever changing disguises. Crowds gathered, masked and disguised, in
public spaces, such as the Haymarket, where balls were organized. The
masquerade attracted upper and lower classes, men and women. It was
unsurpassed in providing a site for intermingling and possibilities for
transgression both socially and sexually. The connection between the
masquerade and the carnivalesque resides in the radical reversal of seemingly fixed social and gender roles, but also in an inevitable return to the
original situation.

The antithetical element that is present in both the masquerade and
the carnivalesque nevertheless moved within certain limits. Masqueraders
did not dress as themselves or as people like themselves, asserts Castle
(1992: 75). But Castle's statement only holds to a certain extent. The
antithetical element would be expressed in reversal of class characteristics
or ethnic backgrounds. As costume historian Aileen Ribeiro shows in *The
Dress Worn at Masquerades in England* (1984), upper-class English ladies
would masquerade as sultanas, not as lower-class Turkish women. So
certain reversals exist up against the maintenance of other class-related
features. Higher classes would dress as shepherds, women as pirates, men
as Dianas. The exotic costume was the most popular subspecies of the
so-called fancy dress, related in particular to those national or ethnic
groups evoking romantic associations. In the masquerade, the Orient was
represented prominently in a profusion of sultans, sultanas, Janissaries,
and Circassian princesses.

Castle interprets the disguise in exotic costume in terms of a utopian
projection and quickly discards motifs focusing on differences in power.

Granted, one might see in foreign costume a mere displacement of
imperialist fantasy; the popularity of the masquerade coincided
after all with the expansion of British imperialism, and the symbolic
joining of races could conceivably be construed as a kind of perverse
allusion to empire. Yet, at a deeper level, such travesties were also
an act of homage—to otherness itself. Stereotypical and inaccurate
though they often were, exotic costumes marked out a kind of
symbolic interpenetration with difference—an almost erotic com-
mingling with the alien. Mimicry became a form of psychological
recognition, a way of embracing, quite literally, the unfamiliar. The
collective result was a utopian projection: the masquerade's visionary
"Congress of Nations"— the image of global conviviality—was
indisputably a thing of fleeting, hallucinatory beauty (Castle 1992:
61–2).

A few features of the masquerade will have become clear by now. Masquerades operate by the grace of mass gatherings whereas cultural cross-dressing seems to point at more individual choices. Choice is, of course, also an issue in a masquerade but its more obvious goal would be the play with different costumes. One could be a Harlequin at one occasion and a sultana at another. Castle's argument that one rubs shoulders with the other, rendering homage to the other in a visionary congress of nations, presupposes an *outside* perspective on the mass of masqueraders. The masqueraders did not agree on nicely distributing different costumes so as to create a utopian vision: this can only be perceived once the masqueraders gathered.

What interests me however is not the element of play as such, but the implied question of power. Who represents whom and why? The carnivalesque and the masquerade with their antithetical characteristics turn the tables on the rich and powerful, but whose tables are turned and by whom when women dress as if they were Oriental women? Who is playing around with cultural roles and who exactly is being played with? My questions suggest a need to refocus on certain aspects that Castle dismisses too hastily: the relations between self and other as they are perceived within hierarchies, and engender them in a sociocultural context.

One might think that the play with cultural roles is obvious, because, in the three turqueries shown, the women who are represented are clearly Western women. But I think that the effort to read "the Occident" in the paintings is as unavailing as the failed attempt to read "the Orient" in them. No sense of categorical purity in the interpretation of cultural cross-dressing can be obtained, although some details might again give us this impression. I am thinking, for instance, about details which occur in the titles. Nattier's *Sultane sortant du bain* is also known as *Mademoiselle de Clermont at the Bath*; Vanloo's *Une sultane prenant du café* acquired the addition "represented with the traits of Madame de Pompadour" (Rosenberg and Cahut 1977). Names of Western women do not exactly jive with the impulse to interpret the women in the paintings as Oriental. However, the changes in titles are more likely to tell us more about accrued histories of interpretation than provide a decisive answer as to who and what is represented.

Illustrative of this apparent interpretational aporia was a response of a friend of mine to whom I showed these cultural cross-dressers. He remarked "They are not supposed to represent harem women, are they?" The ambivalence he expressed reflects exactly what I will try to argue in the rest of this article, that is, the representations of cultural cross-dressing do put into question fixed notions of cultural identities and pose a situation of negotiation: the exchange for which I argued earlier. Reading only Orientalness or Westernness in the paintings is difficult to achieve, but the resulting ambiguity serves to maintain a fine line between two possibilities, equally unsuitable: the representation of European women posing as Oriental women, and a complete conflation between Oriental and Western. In other words, cultural cross-dressing has to reveal itself *as such*, while simultaneously perpetuating the illusion and desire to "be" an Oriental woman. The *desirability* to "be" this other woman is absolutely necessary. But not just any other kind of other woman functions in the same way. The representation of French women as black women is to my knowledge non-existent, at least with respect to eighteenth-century representations. The tension between these two poles of revealing and maintenance of illusion brings about the play, in addition to the ambivalent dialogue present in the paintings. Therefore, I propose not to take as the theme of the representations either cultural cross-dressing revealing itself as such, or the perpetuation of the illusion, but to read the depictions of cultural cross-dressing as intersecting sign systems in which a situation of negotiation is emblematized.

Exchanging Information, Negotiating Power

To illustrate my point let us look at the two Vanloo paintings *Une sultane prenant du café* and *Deux sultanes travaillant à la tapisserie*. Madame de Pompadour commissioned Carle Vanloo, a very fashionable painter in France in the mid-eighteenth century, to execute the two paintings, so-called *dessus-de-porte*, for her Turkish-style room in the Château de Bellevue. The relation between the two paintings is emphasized in both their function and their subject matter. The *dessus-de-porte* were commissioned as pendants. Traditionally, pendants were pairs of paintings, often portraits, that were related in their representation or were meant to indicate a mutual bond. The subject matter of the two canvasses is related in the repetition of various elements, most notably the window, the flowers, and the negotiation going on between the women in both paintings.

The window seems to be the same in both paintings, although it is taken at closer range in *Deux sultanes*, and functions as the source of light in both. Its presence indicates the division between the outside world and the interior scene that we as spectators perceive. The window functions as a framing device, seemingly overdetermining the message. Because the window is explicitly included in the scene, it emphasizes even more our awareness of being inside.

Yet another issue is addressed by the window in combination with the flowers in the pendants. In *Une sultane prenant du café* the woman seated on the right wears flowers on her headdress and a vase containing flowers is placed on the windowsill. Although the flowers are natural, in both instances of their use in the painting they have been cut. As we know, cut flowers quickly fade. They fade almost as rapidly as the flowers of the bindweed discussed earlier. And their wilting beauty might reflect back upon the woman wearing the flowers on her headdress in the painting.[4] Cut flowers also signify cultivation, as the still life-like arrangement of the flowers in the vase suggests. The relation with still life painting is reinforced in the combination of different flowers in the vase, a common-place established through Dutch still life painting of the seventeenth century (Bryson 1990).

The position of the vase in the windowsill, inside, but next to the window indicating the dividing screen between inside and outside, focuses our attention on the "cultivatedness" of the flowers. By extension, it also points to the "cultivatedness" of the person wearing the flowers on her headdress. This element of cultivation is repeated in *Deux sultanes* through the transposition of the world beyond the windowpane into the flowers in the tapestry and the flower and leaf motifs on the cushions and drapery. In general, I want to suggest that both paintings pose the question of inside versus outside, in terms of that of culture versus nature.

The situation of negotiation in both paintings questions this apparent set of rigid oppositions. In *Une sultane* an arrested moment is depicted—not any moment in time, however, but the exact point in time at which an exchange takes place. By the title, which enhances the legibility of the painting, we are alerted to this particular situation. The negotiation is represented in the steaming cup of coffee, handed to the sultana by the black woman, and in the look between the two women. Coffee, introduced in the 1660s by the ambassador of the Ottoman sultan, had become a fashionable commodity in French eighteenth-century society, albeit only for its upper-class consumers (Martino 1906: 348). Meanwhile it maintained at least a part of its "outside" property for the French popul-ation at large. There is another quality of coffee that I want to point out. As Edward Lane (1973: 138) in his description of the modern Egyptians indicated, coffee needed careful preparation, both of the beans and of the coffee itself. With reference to Lévi-Strauss' distinction between the raw and the cooked, coffee can be considered not a raw item, but a highly refined commodity (1964).

The coffee cup embodies both inside qualities (a refined cultured com-modity) and outside qualities (a culturally alien element imported into France). As such the window can be aligned with the coffee cup, because each points at the difference between inside and outside, culture and nature. In that respect, the black woman would seem to be firmly placed in the realm of nature, outside the cultivated space depicted. The display of white and black women in paintings has a long tradition.[5] Therein, the roles for both were defined in antithetical ways. Black women were mostly depicted as servants and interpreted as such, white women as mistresses. Black women were represented as active, displaying and adorn-ing their mistresses, as we have also seen in Nattier's painting *Sultane sortant du bain*. This is how oppositions in class and race were repres-ented. In opposition to this binary scheme, I would argue that the black woman occupies a mobile position, an ability to move in both inside and outside spaces. She is part of the interior scene, but she has entered the Oriental space created in this room from outside, while the sultana is maintained within the seclusion of the imaginary harem.

In *Deux sultanes* the negotiation seems less obvious except for the look the two women exchange. Yet, the gestures of the women are significant. The woman on the right leans forward, she extends her hand, and her legs are bent as if to reinforce the argument she tries to convey to the woman on the left. The latter is in a position of listening. She sits more relaxed, while holding the needle for her tapestry work. Interestingly enough, in the engraved version of the painting by Jacques-Firmin Beauvarlet, the title is changed to *La Confidence* (confidence in the sense of to be confidential with someone, usually suggesting erotic secrets).

The significance of the change in the title is that it foregrounds the nature of the exchange: one woman confiding in another. I would suggest that the speech of the woman on the right is reworked at the same moment. This is done by way of the knots the woman on the left ties on the tapestry because she is the only one holding a needle. I base this assertion on work by Nancy Miller on female writers and the tying of knots as a way of writing for women.[6] This reworking and questioning of the nature–culture opposition by way of positing negotiation as a consistent pattern in the paintings leads me again to consider Madame de Pompadour as the cultural cross-dresser in these particular paintings. In the representation of Madame de Pompadour as sultana, it is significant that the painting is a *dessus-de-porte*, marking the boundaries between this room where she "is" a sultana and other spaces where she has other functions. We can say that the Orient is brought home to France as an imaginary "space." Yet we might perhaps see de Pompadour's cultural cross-dressing as inspired by a different motivation: the desire to overcome strict demarcations in function and power.

When we take a look at the position that Madame de Pompadour held as the official royal mistress at the French court of Louis XV it is clear that she occupied a role that was both fixed and transitional. In comparison to the Queen, related to the King by force of an arranged marriage, the official mistress derived her position from his desire. But to maintain her status, which according to Chaussinand-Nogaret is marginal and central at the same time, she will have to continually stimulate the King's desire. As soon as he loses interest, her position will be taken by the next mistress:

> Thus a disequilibrium is created between the queen and the mistress: for the one indifference and respect, for the other love and influence . . . A distribution of roles, a specialization of functions therefore exists between the women of the king. The queen embodies order, legitimacy, orthodoxy, and immobility. The mistress, on the contrary, is pleasure, movement, and creation (Chaussinand-Nogaret 1990: 16).

Madame de Pompadour can therefore be seen as an "in-between" herself, occupying a provisional space between the King and the Queen. It is striking in that light to see her represented as a sultana, the highest position of a woman in the harem of the sultan. Any woman in the harem could become a sultana, a function which does not imply the demarcations between Queen and mistress at the French court. The legitimacy embodied by the Queen—emphasized in her official function of bearing the royal heir—is displaced onto the sultana, who bore the sultan's children. Moreover, the sultanas often played an important part in the political powerplay of the seraglio in which the procuration of their children in the line of succession was but one aspect of the intrigues. Madame de Pompadour's informal political powers at the French court were widely recognized (Boer 1998). Ultimately, the sultana's political role could result in the actual access to power.[7]

Therefore, the ostensible appeal of Madame de Pompadour's acting out desire by representing herself as the personification of the desirable (for the male gaze) is supplemented with the effort of overcoming the strict demarcations in function and power.

Until now we have looked at details in the representations of cultural cross-dressing that indicated and questioned distinctions between inside and outside, between culture and nature. Returning to Nattier's painting *Sultane sortant du bain*, we need to problematize these concepts that are also played out on the body of the woman depicted. If we follow the direction of looking in the image, all eyes focus on the woman who supposedly was Mlle de Clermont, in awe of her beauty. The figure that interests me most is the woman to the right of Mlle de Clermont. She looks intently at a piece of fabric which she holds to dry Mlle de Clermont's feet before she dresses. She looks at the fabric and not at the object of all other looks. By her focus on this narrative element in the painting, the fabric, she emphasizes the process of dressing, and the possibilities to take up "dress." After a bath one can decide how to dress and thus to decide to dress as Oriental, temporarily assuming a different cultural identity. All but one of the looks are directed to Mlle de Clermont, as are ours as spectators. She returns our gaze, however, and forces us to consider what is going on in the painting, that is, to reconsider our easy assumption that this is the Orient displayed before our eyes.[8]

Nattier's painting proposes the question of fixating and fixed notions by explicitly referring to the *process* of dressing and taking up an identity. As I have argued before, the interpretation of cultural cross-dressing is necessarily based on a wavering in-between, where the negotiation of different roles and positions takes place. The point that *Sultane sortant du bain* makes is that it refers to the agency involved both of the cultural cross-dresser and of the spectator looking at a scene of cultural cross-dressing.

What Have Boundaries Got to Do with It?

I want to conclude my argument with a few brief considerations on the importance of the concept of cultural cross-dressing and boundaries as a necessary element for consideration within it. In her study *Vested Interests: Cross-dressing and Cultural Anxiety* (1992), Marjorie Garber states that there can be no culture without the transvestite, because the transvestite marks the entry into the social order. One of Garber's examples is Flora Tristan cross-dressing as a Turkish man in order to gain access into the House of Lords (pp. 314–16). In order to resolve a situation where women were not allowed, Tristan cross-dresses in a double sense, as a man and as a Turk. Appropriating the representation of a cultural "other" she, of course, pulls at the fabric of gender roles. But Turkish dress is utilized here as a mediating third "space," the "space of representation" as Garber following Lacan calls it. However, I am not as optimistic about the automatic effect of cultural cross-dressing and its possibilities for play as Garber. And my hesitation centers around "cultural otherness" as a means to another end. It is very hard to see how cultural otherness can find a space other than its stereotype, unless we theorize it. We need to take into account the problematization of concepts that naturalize those stereotypes. Moreover, it is necessary to realize that cultural cross-dressing is deeply implicated in unequal relations of power, where the cultural "other" does not call the shots and has little or no recourse to influence the process of being represented.

In order to elaborate this aspect of power inequality and take it back to contemporary debates on self and other, let me briefly expand on boundaries. Boundaries have a tendency to be perceived as anonymous and to supersede the individual, as geopolitician Michel Foucher (1991) has argued. Dividing spaces and groups of peoples, yet no one's possession, the anonymity of boundaries is guaranteed by naturalizing impulses that strengthen their stable and immobile qualities. Those naturalizing impulses, I would argue, help to make the human activity in *constructing* boundaries disappear, i.e. the act of boundary-making. As a result, the question of boundaries has been directed toward the definition of *what* a boundary is and *where* it is located.

I will not elaborate on this aspect, but it will be clear that the questions *what* and *where* reinforce fixity, anonymity, and the apparent differential powers of boundaries. It limits possibilities for interpretation and operates as a reductive instrument for those interpretations. Instead, I propose to theorize boundaries as a function and in their functioning. Questions, then, that might be asked go as follows: Who draws up the boundaries? Who takes those boundaries for granted? Who is afraid boundaries get crossed? Who does cross boundaries? Whose boundaries are transgressed? Thus, these questions try to deal with the *how* and *why* of boundary construction.

Boundaries, then, are not stable, but mobile, even more of a "space" of negotiation. It is a space in which different and contrasting visions, more often than not unequal in terms of power, come into play. So boundaries are negotiated in a process that does not stop with the provisional designation of a boundary. The boundary is arbitrary in character, temporary and changeable (Boer 1996b).

This necessary detour about boundaries does lead back to the mixing of ingredients designer Dries van Noten talked about and to the post-modern, near commonplace, of a boundaryless world. If only that were true! If hybridity is indeed taken as bricolage, as a mix to your liking, then we might ask whether it is worthwhile to spend time analyzing fashion or cultural cross-dressing. But if, in contrast, we take Gayatri Spivak's statement seriously that "radical alterity requires imaging," (Conference Modern European Images of the Other, Bergen, Norway, October 1996) then we might as well scrutinize those images critically and carefully consider what negotiations take place, if any.[9]

A well-known advertisement of United Colors of Benetton shows three hearts titled *White, Black, Yellow,* and thus takes us further than skin deep or what covers the body. At the heart of the matter, the advertisement proposes, we are all equal; no boundaries, no negotiations, so step into the parlor of sameness. But hybridity as an active moment of challenge and resistance against the dominant cultural power does retain and urge a focus on the political, as Homi Bhabha contends. With this focus in mind and cultural cross-dressing as the complex and dynamic process I have been analyzing, I want to turn to my last example.

The Dutch company for men's fashion HIJ (indicating the third person pronoun masculine in Dutch)[10] launched a campaign in the Spring of 1995 (Figure 6) in which a series of six black men were depicted for the promotion of shirts. In a time of crisis on the domestic front in which the Dutch concern about the growing numbers of asylum-seekers entering the country was at its height, the promotional campaign for shirts did not cause a ripple. No comments appeared in the press. When I asked people what this campaign was about—besides clothing—they responded that it must be connected to rap music or to the growing interest in aboriginal art or to a Third-World awareness in general.[11] Note the link with the Benetton advertisements that also promote cross-cultural relations and environmental concerns. Half of the photos were similar in content to the photo of the black man in Figure 6: men wearing shirts, the patterns of which were repeated on their faces. The other half showed black men bared to the skin except for some beads and feather ornaments around their ankles and wrists that "dressed" them. They were carrying shields, hoops in which the shirts were hung in such a way that they functioned quite coyly as modern-day fig leaves. The overall image of the campaign was "men as warriors." Warriors who were in dire need of a reconstruction and rehabilitation of their masculinity which was to be attained through black men as a sign.

This clever device might be interpreted as a form of ethno-marketing, targeting a consumer public of young black men. But what struck me most was the excess of the message, the overflow of the print of the shirts onto the faces of the men in the imagery. Whereas clothing is removable and positioned on the body, the print indicates forms of inscription *onto* the body that have much more serious implications. The signifiers of

Figure 6
HIJ ad. Public advertisement,
The Netherlands, Spring 1995.
Permission by WE company.

racial, ethnic and cultural boundaries will, of course, in this instance not
carry over onto the men buying the shirts. For potential buyers the shirt
will be a detachable piece of clothing, the paint on the faces of the black
men "belongs" there. The new, probably white, masculine warrior will
make do with the shirt only.[12]

Fashion, in conclusion, produces, promotes, and recycles powerful
images of otherness. I am highly critical of some forms of cultural cross-
dressing, without wanting to dismiss its vital and integral role in the

fashion system. My critique is aimed at the lack of political awareness about the implications of the fundamentally contradictory character of cultural cross-dressing. However, I believe, perhaps naively so, in the possibility of becoming sensitized to the mechanisms at work in cultural cross-dressing; these mechanisms include possibilities for negotiating the inequalities of power, and undermining the naturalizing impulses that strengthen them by taking the functioning of boundaries into account. Then the dictum "Just a fashion" will have run its course.

Acknowledgments

I have benefited greatly from discussions of previous versions of this article in Groningen and Maastricht, The Netherlands, Rochester, NY and Bergen, Norway. I am grateful to my anonymous reviewer at *Fashion Theory* for drawing out the implications of my argument and for providing me with additional references.

Notes

1. For labor conditions in the globalized fashion production process, see Naomi Klein (2001: 202–29).
2. Such historical explanations have been foregrounded by Pape (1989), Breukink-Peeze (1989) and Martino (1906).
3. I differ here from a more strict interpretation by Joanna Entwistle (2000) about fashion as a sign system.
4. One of the persistent stereotypes about women in the Orient occurring in Orientalist literature is that their beauty quickly fades because of the frequent baths they take.
5. See Linda Nochlin (1989), Griselda Pollock (1999) and Mieke Bal (1993) for critical analyses of this artistic tradition.
6. Nancy K. Miller has analyzed the relation between tying knots and women as writers (1988: 125–62). For the relation between the braiding of hair and the exchange of information see Boer (1996a, forthcoming: chapter 2).
7. For analyses of the political role of the sultana, see Shaw (1976: 170, 191, 193–4, 204), Mernissi (1990), and Peirce (1993).
8. See for a slightly different analysis of this painting, Pollock (1999: 287–94).
9. For an extended analysis of postmodern fashion and the place of women in the history of textile, see Spivak (1999: 337–52).
10. The company used to have separate stores for HIJ (him) and ZIJ (her), until the company merged the two into WE in 1999.
11. For the connections between rap, masculinity and black men, see Andrew Ross (1998: 71–8).

12. It might be clear from my analysis that I am at odds with Pacteau's
fascinating interpretation of Jean-Paul Goude's photos of Grace
Jones (Pacteau 1994: 123–43). What is detachable there according
to Pacteau, the black skin, is exactly what cannot be detached in
the HIJ advertisement. I am grateful to the publisher's anonymous
reviewer for referring me to this aspect of Pacteau's analysis.

References

Apter, Emily. 1999. *Continental Drift: From National Characters to
Virtual Subjects*. Chicago, IL and London: The University of Chicago
Press.

Bal, Mieke. 1993. "His Master's Eye." In David Micheal Levin (ed.),
Modernity and the Hegemony of Vision, pp. 379–404. Berkeley, CA:
University of California Press.

Barthes, Roland. 1967. *Le système de la mode*. Paris: Editions du Seuil.

Boer, Inge. E. 1994. "This is not the Orient: Theory and Postcolonial
Practice." In Mieke Bal and Inge E. Boer (eds), *The Point of Theory:
Practices in Cultural Analysis*, pp. 210–19. New York and Amsterdam:
Continuum and Amsterdam University Press.

—— . 1996a. "Despotism from under the Veil: Masculine and Feminine
Readings of the Despot and the Harem." *Cultural Critique* 32,4:
43–73.

—— . 1996b. "The World Beyond our Window: Nomads, Travelling
Theories and the Function of Boundaries." *Parallax: A Journal of
Metadiscursive Theory and Cultural Practices* (Sp. Issue Dissonant
Feminisms) 1,3: 7–26.

—— . 1998. "Culture as a Gendered Battleground: The Patronage of
Madame de Pompadour." In Tjitske Akkerman and Siep Stuurman
(eds), *Perspectives on Feminist Political Thought in European History:
From the Middle Ages to the Present*, pp. 104–21. London: Routledge.

—— . Forthcoming. *Disorienting Vision: Rereading Stereotypes in French
Orientalist Texts and Images*.

Breukink-Peeze, Margaret. 1989. "Eene fraaie kleding, van den turkschen
dragt ontleent. Turkse kleding en mode à la turque in Nederland." In
Hans Theunissen, Annelies Abelman and Wim Meulenkamp (eds),
Topkapi & Turkomanie: Turks-Nederlandse ontmoetingen sinds 1600,
pp. 130–40. Amsterdam: De Bataafsche Leeuw.

Bryson, Norman. 1990. *Looking at the Overlooked: Four Essays on Still
Life Painting*. Cambridge, MA and London: Harvard University Press.

—— . 1994. "Art in Context." In Mieke Bal and Inge E. Boer (eds), *The
Point of Theory: Practices of Cultural Analysis*, pp. 66–78. New York
and Amsterdam: Continuum and Amsterdam University Press.

Castle, Terry. 1992. *Masquerade and Civilization: The Carnivalesque in
Eighteenth-Century English Culture and Fiction*. London: Methuen.

Chaussinand-Nogaret, Guy. 1990. *La vie quotidienne des femmes du roi: D'Agnès Sorel à Marie-Antoinette*. Paris: Hachette.

Culler, Jonathan. 1988. *Framing the Sign: Criticism and Its Institutions*. Norman, OK and London: University of Oklahoma Press.

Dekker, Rudolf and Lotte van de Pol. 1989. *The Tradition of Female Transvestism in Early Modern Europe*. London: MacMillan Press and New York: St. Martin's Press.

Entwistle, Joanna. 2000. *The Fashioned Body: Fashion, Dress and Modern Social Theory*. Cambridge: Polity Press.

Foucher, Michel. 1991. "Frontières à retracer: un point de vue de géo-politicien." In *Frontières et limites*, pp. 69–81. Paris: Editions du Centre Pompidou.

Garber, Marjorie. 1992. *Vested Interests: Cross-Dressing and Cultural Anxiety*. New York and London: Routledge.

Klein, Naomi. 2001. *No Logo*. London: Flamingo.

Lane, Edward W. 1973 (1836). *An Account of the Manners and Customs of the Modern Egyptians*, Edward Stanley Poole (ed.), introduction by Jon Manchip White. New York: Dover Publications.

Lévi-Strauss, Claude. 1964. *Le cru et le cuit*. Paris: Plon.

Martino, Pierre. 1906. *L'Orient dans la littérature française au XVIIe et au XVIIIe siècle*. Paris: Hachette.

Mernissi, Fatima. 1990. *Sultanes oubliées: Femmes chefs d'Etat en Islam*. Paris: Albin Michel.

Miller, Nancy K. 1988. "The Knot, the Letter, and the Book." In *Subject to Change: Reading Feminist Writing*, pp. 125–62. New York: Columbia University Press.

Nochlin, Linda. 1989. "The Imaginary Orient." In *The Politics of Vision: Essays on Nineteenth-Century Art and Society*, pp. 33–60. New York: Harper and Row, Publishers.

Ockman, Carol. 1995. *Ingres's Eroticized Bodies: Retracing the Serpentine Line*. New Haven, CT and London: Yale University Press.

Pacteau, Francette. 1994. *The Symptom of Beauty*. London: Reaktion Books.

Pape, Marie Elisabeth. 1989. "Turquerie im 18. Jahrhundert und des 'Receuil Ferriol.'" In Gereon Sievernich and Hendrik Budde (eds), *Europa und der Orient 800–1900*, pp. 305–24. Gütersloh and München: Bertelsmann Lexicon Verlag.

Peirce, Leslie P. 1993. *The Imperial Harem: Women and Sovereignty in the Ottoman Empire*. Oxford: Oxford University Press.

Pollock, Griselda. 1999. *Differencing the Canon: Feminist Desire and the Writing of Art's Histories*. London and New York: Routledge.

Ribeiro, Aileen. 1984. *The Dress Worn at Masquerades in England, 1730 to 1790, and the Relation to Fancy Dress in Portraiture*. New York and London: Garland Publishing.

Roche, Daniel. 1989. *La culture des apparences: Une histoire du vêtement (XVIIe–XVIIIe siècle)*. Paris: Fayard, Collection Po.

Rosenberg, Pierre and Marie-Christine Cahut. 1977. *Carle Vanloo: Premier peintre du roi*. Nice: Musée Chéret.

Ross, Andrew. 1998. "The Gangsta and the Diva." In *Real Love: In Pursuit of Cultural Justice*, pp. 71–8. New York and London: New York University Press.

Russo, Mary. 1986. "Female Grotesques: Carnival and Theory." In Teresa de Laurentis (ed.), *Feminist Studies/Critical Studies*, pp. 213–30. Bloomington, IN: Indiana University Press.

Shaw, Stanford J. 1976. *History of the Ottoman Empire and Modern Turkey*. Vol. 1. Cambridge: Cambridge University Press.

Spivak, Gayatri Chakravorty. 1999. *A Critique of Postcolonial Reason: Toward a History of the Vanishing Present*. Cambridge, MA and London: Harvard University Press.

van der Haak, Bregtje. 1996. "Ik ben hard voor mezelf en ook voor anderen." (I am Demanding for Myself and for Others.) *Elle* September 1996: 14.

Young, Robert J. C. 1995. *Colonial Desire: Hybridity, Theory, Culture and Race*. London and New York: Routledge.

Fashion Theory, Volume 6, Issue 4, pp. 441–446
Reprints available directly from the Publishers.
Photocopying permitted by licence only.
© 2002 Berg. Printed in the United Kingdom.

Exhibition Review: "Radical" Fashion? A Critique of the Radical Fashion Exhibition, Victoria and Albert Museum, London

**Reviewed by
Bradley Quinn**

Bradley Quinn is a writer and curator who has worked as a fashion journalist and editor for publications and broadcasters on both sides of the Atlantic. He is the author of *Chinese Style* and his book *Techno Fashion* will be released by Berg Publishers in January 2003.

18 October 2001–6 January 2002

Radicals, visionaries, revolutionaries or outcasts? The boundaries between these terms blurred as the work of eleven contemporary designers was presented in the *Radical Fashion* exhibition at the Victoria and Albert Museum, London. Curated by Claire Wilcox—whose projects include the *Satellites of Fashion* and the *Wear on the Street* exhibitions—the choice of work presented in *Radical Fashion* "marks moments in time, changes in attitudes" (Wilcox 2001: 1). In a catalog essay entitled "I Try Not to Fear Radical Things," Wilcox appropriated the term "radical" to describe the international fashion scene at the beginning of the new millennium.

She asserts that *Radical Fashion* "is fashion in 2001 at its most innovative and visionary, going the full stretch from dream to reality," describing each designer as having "a radical, uncompromising and highly influential approach to fashion" (Wilcox 2001: 1, 6).

"Radical" points to the uncodified, the intractable, the dramatic, even the enchanted—implying rapid changes in ideas and images. Applied to fashion, radical implies a sudden thrill of meanings that themselves quicken, mutate, rupture, fissure, or collapse. Fashion designers working in this vein reshape the body, design according to philosophical and intellectual concerns, push boundaries, challenge perceptions, and usurp conformity to give form to extravagant projects of the imagination. While the concept of radical is a relative term, it becomes indexical when applied to the uncompromising collections of Azzedine Alaïa, Hussein Chalayan, Comme des Garçons, Jean-Paul Gaultier, Helmut Lang, Alexander McQueen, Martin Margiela, Issey Miyake, Junya Watanabe, Vivienne Westwood, and Yohji Yamamoto. But many of these designers' signature oeuvres were passed over in a choice of garments that defined radical through the intellectual equivalent of negative space.

The exhibitions and presentations that engage the public in the interpretation of dress traditionally tend to surround the spectator with representations of beauty, elegance, high design, and prestige. These institutional presentations of the discipline often disguise fashion as a culture where only aesthetic goals are central, without revealing that fashion is also a realm heavily freighted with contradictions, dualities, defiance, and subversive ideas. Therefore, an exhibition premised on antithetical elements of fashion promises to present a forward-thinking step towards showcasing the type of works designers themselves regard as innovative and cutting edge, decoding the messages of resistance and dissent voiced in their garments. *Radical Fashion*, despite its appealing remit, neither unmasked nor interpreted the radical dimensions commonly associated with most of these eleven designers, downplaying the extremes evoked by the concept of radical or ignoring them altogether.

From the point of the spectator, the declarations of radicalism alluded to in the exhibition's gripping title heightened expectations of its content and cued how the exhibition should be interpreted. This suggested that the subject of *Radical Fashion* was not necessarily a presentation of fashion *per se*, but an appraisal of the tropes accessed via the language of fashion. With its inherent ambiguities and pluralistic definitions, fashion offers a domain where justification is unnecessary and often inappropriate. However, the choice of garments exhibited in *Radical Fashion* often worked against its theme, inciting visitors to the exhibition to evaluate what could actually be understood in the literal context of "radical" fashion. Far from blowing the cobwebs off conventional presentations of dress, *Radical Fashion* cocooned itself in surprisingly bland choices of silhouettes that undermined the impact of all that the term radical conveys. Many garments were selected from collections spanning a decade, in opposition to the exhibit's remit to showcase "fashion in 2001" (Wilcox 2001: 6). Most of these seemed outdated, or lacked any discernible contemporary "edge" at all.

Radical Fashion surveyed the 1990s but cut its chronology short of some of fashion's true radicalism. Westwood's punk era, one of the most pivotal movements expressed in contemporary fashion, seemed to have dissolved and re-formed as oversized denim. Westwood's insight into fetishism and her ingenious reversal of underwear as outerwear were ignored in favor of dresses tailored from vast panels of fabric. Gaultier, who brought the raw sex appeal of his conical bustiers and fetishistic corsetry to the Paris catwalk while making shocking attempts to transform the skirt into a menswear item, was represented in evening-gown silhouettes and unassuming garments. Azzedine Alaïa, a designer best known for his spiraling zippers and the fetish dresses popularized by Grace Jones, was largely represented by demure dresses trimmed in lace, embroidery, and beading. By bringing sex to the catwalk, each of these designers introduced alternative visions of sex appeal that offered women choices beyond the cliché of the sexy skirt and the plunging neckline. However, the eroticism of explicit garments and the impact of sexuality on the notion of radical was not addressed in the exhibition.

Issey Miyake, famous for his reversal of proportions and deconstructed tailoring, was represented by works from his newly established APOC (A Piece of Cloth) range (2000). Ultimately, Miyake intends to use vending machines to sell generic garments stitched into tubes of fabric. While the catalog essay interpreted this project as an enterprise that "takes radicalism to a new height," many of his contemporaries are highly critical of his unexpected foray into this venture of commercialization and mass production, and his move away from the radicalism that characterized his work for decades (Wilcox 2001: 2).

While Junya Watanabe's clothes were radical in their geometric textures and undulating forms, Rei Kawakubo's Comme des Garçons contributions were less so. The proximity of two designers virtually indistinguishable in their ideology and aesthetics diluted the impact of their respective works, effectively rationalizing them into a single exhibit (the catalog bills them both under the rubric of Comme des Garçons). Had one of them been omitted, might there have been room for the pioneering work of John Galliano? Or the radical talents and innovative designs of Thierry Mugler, whose corsets place motorcycle headlights between the breasts and provide the wearer with chrome handlebars with which to steer herself. As two of contemporary fashion's true radicals, Galliano's and Mugler's work was conspicuous in its absence.

True to his radical spirit, the "Red-Glass Slide and Ostrich Feather Dress" made by Alexander McQueen (*Voss*, Spring/Summer 2001) exemplified the theme of the exhibition. The lower half of the dress is made from ostrich feathers that expand outwards into a crinoline-like shape, while the upper part of the dress is constructed from two thousand microscope

Figure 1
The "Red-Glass Slide and Ostrich Feather Dress" from McQueen's *Voss* collection (spring/summer 2001) exemplified the "Radical" theme. Here, McQueen destabilizes the usual affinity between fashion and material—inverting the sensual relationhip that invites both wearer and observer to touch, feel and stroke the sumptuous textures characteristic of dress fabric. By using non-traditional materials that have rough, sharp, and even dangerous surfaces, McQueen drives the observer away, maintaining critical distance from the wearer. Photography by Chris Moore, from *Radical Fashion*, V&A, 2001.

slides layered from hipbone to throat. Ordered from a surgical supplier, each slide was hand-drilled and individually painted red to suggest scrutinizing the body under a microscope. The dress also inverts the relationship between the visual and the tactile, the surface and the visceral; senses often associated with distance and nearness, respectively. As the dress replaces the tactile characteristics of fabric with segments of glass that could instantly shatter into a cascading razor's edge, the seductive materials that caress the skin are supplanted by shards that slice it open. McQueen wants to get a closer look at the body, even going beneath its surface. Employing the microscope as an agent of technology to do this invokes the power that science ultimately has over the body. Pleasure and pain, life and death are inexorably linked to science; once in its control the body can be penetrated to look within it.

Forming a part of Hussein Chalayan's presentation, a film projection brought his *Ventriloquy* collection (Spring/Summer 2001) to life in an animated version of a "space invaders" video game, in which the models accrued points by breaching the shells of each other's dresses, "shooting" each other until the last survivor became the victor. Chalayan's film presentation heralded a move away from static dress forms and live models, providing a platform to showcase experimental designs or tangential projects cinematically that a designer may not be able to explore in a live show.

In many respects *Radical Fashion* encapsulated almost everything that is frustratingly unradical in the British fashion establishment, producing the climate that Westwood, Chalayan, and McQueen decamped to Paris to avoid. In an industry almost completely lacking a couture tradition, the British Fashion Council praises the inventiveness and edginess of its designers, celebrating their innovation but never encouraging it, routinely rejecting applications that suggest a radical move forward. Designers showing on the official Fashion Week schedule are restricted to conventional catwalk presentations, as the British Fashion Council does not recognize cinematic presentation or art installations as legitimate fashion shows. Added to that, few picture editors of British newspapers will publish film stills or photographs of a film installation in the fashion pages.

In the meta-category of fashion, the line between the rational and the ridiculous becomes muted as the difference between radical and innovative is confused. Those outside the British fashion establishment regard this paradox as an evolving hallmark of British fashion. As innovative becomes "Innovative" and radical becomes "Radical," the fashion establishment seem to move further away from the cutting-edge reputation formed by British visionaries. Despite the acclaim received by fashion's radicals abroad, these aspects of their work are clearly undervalued in Britain. *Radical Fashion*, in its juxtaposition of British fashion with other international designers, brought these values into a broader contextual framework that highlighted the emerging trend to rationalize contemporary fashion on several levels. Perhaps the British fashion establishment tries to fear radical things after all?

References

Wilcox, Claire. 2001. "I Try Not to Fear Radical Things." In *Radical Fashion*. London: V&A Publications.

Fashion Theory, Volume 6, Issue 4, pp. 447–450
Reprints available directly from the Publishers.
Photocopying permitted by licence only.
© 2002 Berg. Printed in the United Kingdom.

**Reviewed by
Valerie Steele**

Book Review

***Footnotes: On Shoes*. Edited by Shari Benstock and Suzanne Ferriss (Rutgers University Press, 2001) 325 pages**

***Women's Shoes in America, 1795–1930* by Nancy E. Rexford (The Kent State University Press, 2000) 393 pages**

Shoes exert a powerful fascination. As *Footnotes* demonstrates, there is a bit of Imelda Marcos even in the notoriously dowdy academic community. This collection of fourteen essays goes beyond traditional costume history to explore the significance of shoes in art, dance, film, literature, social history, and contemporary society. The book is not quite as interdisciplinary as one might hope, however, since the majority of the contributors are professors of English, literature, and/or women's studies. Most teach in the United States, and the others are based in Canada and Great Britain. The quality of the essays varies, but, at their best, they are excellent.

Gender and sexuality are the focus of many of the essays in the book, from Christopher Breward's "Fashioning Masculinity" to Jaime Hovey's "In Rebecca's Shoes: Lesbian Fetishism in Daphne Du Maurier's *Rebecca.*" But perhaps the most trenchant is Lorraine Gammon's analysis of the appeal of "sexy girl shoes," which asks the question, "What's at stake? Female fetishism or narcissism?" The co-author of *Female Fetishism*, Gammon has a thorough grasp of the complex theoretical issues involved in women's ambivalent love affair with shoes: female objectification, the fragmentation of the body, the masquerade of femininity, femininity as perversion, commodity fetishism, and the ways in which female narcissism and fetishism are articulated through consumerism. In order to understand women's shoe fetishism, Gammon suggests, we need to think less about the missing phallus and more about the role of narcissism in fashion.

A number of essays focus on cultural differences. For example, Tace Hendrick's "Are You a Pure Latina?" is a theoretically rigorous, yet also accessible essay that deals with the "mystique" that high heels seem to hold for Latinas. Obviously, not every Latina (Cuban-American or Puerto Rican) or Chicana (Mexican-American) wears high heels constantly, but, as Hendrick points out, "popular self-representations of a certain kind of Latina femininity include a negotiated acceptance of certain stereotypes." What interests her is "not just the cultural marker of high heels . . . for a certain way of imagining *Latinidad*," but also "how style . . . comes to be the site for contradictory impulses toward femininity and ethnicity."

Julia Emberley, author of *The Cultural Politics of Fur*, is represented here by a brilliant essay on learning to theorize with shoes at the Bata Shoe Museum. Through a close analysis of several exhibitions on shoes, and drawing on Fredric Jameson's theories on postmodernism, she demonstrates that the museum's approach calls into question "the boundary between *shoe as commodity* and *shoe as cultural or aesthetic artifact.*" She focuses especially on "two intersecting orders of difference—cultural difference and sexual difference—that inform the pedagogical rationality of the . . . exhibitions." In the process, she trenchantly critiques the way the museum's history of shoes implies a progressive movement from "functional primitivism to the aesthetic maturity of the civilising process."

In her powerful essay, "Empty Shoes," Ellen Carol Jones looks at the Holocaust through the mute testimony of thousands of pairs of shoes, which were confiscated from the victims of the death camps. Eyewitnesses and survivors recall the horrible significance of shoes during the Third

Reich: "We were shaken to the depths of our soul when the first transport of children's shoes arrived." The very presence of the shoes was, of course, contingent on the absence, the extermination, of those who once wore them. Today 4,000 of these shoes from the death camp at Majdanek are on display at the United States Holocaust Memorial Museum. While acknowledging the problematic aestheticization of history that museum visitors experience, Jones ultimately agrees with the poet Moses Schulstein, who writes: "We are the shoes, we are the last witnesses."

Janice West considers the meaning of shoes in art, analyzing works such as Vincent Van Gogh's *A Pair of Boots* (1886) and Andy Warhol's *Diamond Dust Shoes* (1980). She also discusses shoe paintings by contemporary artists Jim Dine and Lisa Milroy, although, disappointingly, she does not illustrate them. Maureen Turim is more generous with illustrations in her essay on cinema, gender, and footwear. She discusses a wide range of films from *The Gay Shoe Clerk* (1903) to Almodovar's *High Heels* (1996), addressing, albeit briefly, issues such as the close-up and the fetish, the gender of shoes, the heels of the modern woman, fantasies of shoes and dance, the contrast between the shoe and the bare foot, and the man in heels. She analyzes, for example, the use of metonymy in the famous Odessa Steps sequence in *Battleship Potemkin* (1927), which includes shots of a wealthy woman in high heels standing next to a legless beggar, the boots of a Czarist soldier, a woman who snags her heel on the steps and falls, and a child's hand crushed by the shoe of a fleeing man.

Footnotes could usefully be incorporated into a number of college courses devoted to cultural studies or women's studies, as well as fashion studies, per se. Nancy Rexford's *Women's Shoes in America, 1795–1930* is a very different type of book with a very different intended audience. Written by a traditional costume historian, it is divided into two sections. The first, comprising six chapters, is a narrative history of shoes in America. The second (and more interesting) section is organized along the same principle that governs books on identifying, say, species of birds. It is divided into subsections based on easily defined visible characteristics, such as shoes that lace as opposed to shoes that buckle. Essentially a detailed reference work for dating shoes, it will be particularly useful for curators, dealers, collectors, and re-enactors. Indeed, the book has already been awarded a prize by the Costume Society of America.

Fashion Theory, Volume 6, Issue 4, pp. 451–452
Reprints available directly from the Publishers.
Photocopying permitted by licence only.

**Reviewed by
Patrizia Calefato**

Book Review

***Mode in Italy* by Simona Segre, Guerini Scientifica, Milan, 1999**

Simona Segre, social anthropologist, full Professor at Milan IULM, University of Foreign Languages and Communication, and consultant in the fields of marketing and communications, tackles in her versatile work on the history of Italian fashion those phenomena that have occurred over the last fifteen years. She analyzes the metamorphosis of the female body, several myths (including that of jeans), the world of marketing and the concept of fashion as "the Esperanto of contemporaneousness". She researches this concept in depth and traces it back to its roots. The word "fashion", the author states, has not always been an indicator of ways of dressing: customs, clothes, hair-styles, decorations and body changes have had different justifications throughout history, such as sacred or ritual ones, not necessarily linked to the system of social rules that we associate with the word fashion. Only during the Italian Renaissance did elements such as profanity, worldliness and ephemerality, which are typical of fashion phenomena, start to characterize and rule the history of fashion and customs, following varying cycles.

This "Italian" root of the very concept of fashion itself leads the author to consider the Italian case with extreme attention, as it is such an important aspect of culture, economy, creativity and art, even though it was considered a "minor" form of art for a long time, and, above all, linked to craftsmanship. The author states that even though the word "fashion" was imported to Italy from France and even though France was historically the very beating heart of fashionable modernity, Italian traditions boast their own original characteristics. Ever since 1923, the year that witnessed the foundation of the Ente Nazionale della Moda (the National Fashion Organization), the success of "made in Italy" started to take shape. However, only in the post-war period did it start to become a reality with the unforgettable creations of "tailors and dressmakers" (in those days there was no such thing as "designers") such as Simonetta, Carosa, the Fontana sisters, Biki, Schubert and Jole Veneziani, who managed to successfully compete on the international arena with the most prestigious Parisian names in fashion.

This formed the origins of more recent history and includes the basic institution of *ready-to-wear* in the 1950s and 1960s, to which Italian fashion owes a great part of its international success. These years were then followed by the crucial years of "anti-fashion" linked to the dissent movement, and in the 1980s by the explosion of made in Italy. The author pinpoints three different attitudes towards fashion among the Italians at the end of the twentieth century: the years of "intrusive" consumption, i.e. the decade of the "designer label" and the "amoral" 1980s; the years of "insolent" fashion in the 1990s, characterized by *grunge*, minimalism, revivals and the criticism of *fashion victims*; and finally, the years of "expressive" fashion, at the end of the 1990s, based on the aesthetics of consumption, body seduction and "style-mixes".

This book reveals the ways in which fashion becomes a more and more complex and emblematic means of communicating a "national identity" within a global market of both goods and symbols. It leaves open the question of scenarios of the immediate future, which are already visible in the present: how can the social reproduction of fashion images and signs go on being "eurocentric" or "italocentric"?

Fashion Theory, Volume 6, Issue 4, pp. 453–456
Reprints available directly from the Publishers.
Photocopying permitted by licence only.

**Reviewed by
Lynn Sorge**

Book Review

The Corset: A Cultural History by Valerie Steele. New Haven: Yale University Press, 2001

Valerie Steele's book is a welcome addition to a subject of dress history about which far too little has been written. Lavishly illustrated and written in a style accessible to both casual readers and those with more scholarly pursuits, Steele has gathered together for the first time in one place evidence pertaining to disparate discourses on stays and corsets, carefully analyzing them from a cultural history perspective.

Treating her subject broadly, Steele uses a thematic approach to address commonly held notions about "bodies," stays and corsets, while cleverly incorporating into her text the chronological development of style and form of these ubiquitous foundation garments from the late Renaissance into the twentieth century. Setting out to re-examine and challenge accepted thinking about corsets as reflective of female oppression and instruments of patriarchy, Steele begins by tracing the origins of "whalebone bodies" to Spain or Italy in the first half of the sixteenth century, convincingly dispelling the myth that they began in the ancient world. She holds bodies and stays up as courtly and aristocratic garments linked to respectability and physical self-control, therein depicting them as garments mainly of the upper classes until well into the eighteenth century. Although she discusses briefly those of the lower classes, she notes that stays had not worked their way down the social scale until into the nineteenth century when they began to be mass-produced. Steele does not discuss in any kind of depth eighteenth-century stays worn by the lower sorts, and in this omission, has perhaps inadvertently overlooked the very important work done by Beverly Lemire who identified in probate inventories vast quant-ities of ready-made stays intended for the low end of the market as early as 1667 (Lemire 1997: 62, 63).

Steele addresses a number of important points, however, concisely and clearly, including the wearing of corsets by males in the nineteenth century. One of Steele's strengths as an historian lies in her ability to analyze and decipher iconography in visual sources, and to tease out meaning in textual sources. Her theories that works within the genre of "la toilette galante" in the eighteenth century were perceived as being erotic, that nineteenth-century prints of corseted bodies served as surrogates for the nude body, and that lacing and unlacing the corset functioned as symbols of sexual intercourse, are new and fascinating ideas. Her reading of corset advertisements, including her identification of subliminal messages within them, is equally enlightening, and her chapter on the medical effects of nineteenth-century corsets is well researched and carefully written. While she has shown several medical ideas to be conflated with notions of morality, her perceptive analyses of medical effects in general have been rendered even more credible because of her close association with a medical doctor upon whom she relied for interpretation. While she does dispel several notions about the ill effects of the corset, she finds that some of them bear a note of verity and are with foundation. Presenting both sets of evidence in this way exemplifies Steele's unbiased interpretation of her findings in the book overall.

She presents a balanced account of tight-lacing while arguing against the conclusions other researchers have drawn. She believes that most published letters decrying the discomfort of tight-lacing were the work of sexual fantasists and not the expressions of Victorian schoolgirls; she also presents evidence gleaned from artifacts that most corset waists were larger than the mythical sixteen or eighteen inches, therein demonstrating empirically that ". . . object-based research provides unique insights into the historic and aesthetic development of fashion" (Steele 1998: 327). It is only during the last few pages in this chapter, however, that Steele analyses her evidence within the wider context of contemporary society's attitudes to women. This is an intriguing line of thinking which ends all too quickly. Perhaps time or length constraints came into play here, and after all, one cannot do everything in one volume, but to have presented an even broader cultural analysis of the consequences of perceptions of tight-lacing in Victorian society would have been helpful, particularly as Steele is an historian so clearly able to discern meaning and encapsulate it with erudition.

Her cultural analysis comes into its own in the closing two chapters of the book, however, where she discusses other erotic associations of corsetry as seen and read, presents her concept of the Victorian corseted female body as masculinized, discusses the demise of the corset and rise and evolution of other undergarments in the twentieth century, as well as body shaping and sculpting through diet, exercise and corrective surgery. Leaving no stone unturned, she discusses the use and design of corsets in the modern age, spanning punk culture to the catwalk. She argues convincingly here and throughout the book that corsetry conveys now, as it has done in the past, a multiplicity of meanings for both wearers and observers, and that what was once viewed as a symbol of female oppression has now come to be seen as a sign of female empowerment.

In many ways Steele's book is a tour de force. Addressing corsets from the broadest possible perspective within the largest geographical area and across all of history must have been a daunting task, and could have resulted in an unwieldy book. But Steele has cleverly tamed her subject, and in gathering together evidence from disparate visual and textual sources, and from a wide variety of secondary works, she has created a full, culturally unbiased picture of corsets throughout history. It is unfortunate that she was unable to incorporate more primary sources, but given the breadth of her project, this might have been impossible. While the book will be invaluable to dress historians and students of fashion history and theory, it is sure to be of interest also to art, cultural and medical historians, as well as to sociologists, anthropologists and psychologists.

References

Lemire, Beverly. 1997. *Dress, Culture and Commerce: The English Clothing Trade before the Factory, 1660–1800.* Basingstoke: Macmillan Press Ltd.

Steele, Valerie. 1998. "A Museum of Fashion is More Than a Clothes-Bag." *Fashion Theory: The Journal of Dress, Body & Culture*, 2 (4): 327–335.

Fashion Theory, Volume 6, Issue 4, pp. 457–462
Reprints available directly from the Publishers.
Photocopying permitted by licence only.

**Reviewed by
Jennifer Craik**

Book Review

**Out of Line: Australian Women and Style by Margaret
Maynard (UNSW Press, 2001)**

While intriguing, the title of this book might sound like a paradox. Stylish
Australian women? Is it possible? Visitors to Australia have variously
described Australian women's dress sense as dog-eared, loud, vulgar,
favoring comfort over style—at best, imitative, at worst, inferior. But, in
her ground-breaking book, Maynard challenges these perceptions along
with the ambivalent discourses surrounding them. Instead, she argues
that Australian fashion and dress sense should be seen in its own terms.
While it may be true that Australian fashion has largely followed trends
elsewhere, Maynard contends that a distinctive sense of Australian style

has emerged out of the inflection of local conditions, life styles and cultural preoccupations into modes of dress. In short, she argues, Australian fashion is "out of line:"

> Australian fashionable style for women is different, identifiable and should now be redefined as something that is frequently resistant to Eurocentric mainstream ideas. It is gracefully, if not wilfully, "out of line" (p. 13).

While I would agree with the first proposition—that Australian women's fashion is distinctive and identifiable—I would hesitate to endorse the second—that it is "out of line." The very term retains the relativism and normative critique of Australian fashion in comparison with European yardsticks. Instead, we might propose the question: in what ways has Australian style developed an authentic rationale that encapsulates its post-colonial heritage and addresses its national character? This prompts a related question: how can we define a national sense of style?

To answer these questions, it is useful to compare Maynard's book with earlier analyses of Australian fashion (Joel 1998; Martyn 1976; Maynard 1994) and to similar analyses of two other former British dominions[1] that historically transplanted European dress sense—Canada (Routh 1993) and New Zealand (Wolfe 2001). These dominions differed from other colonies where European dress competed—or at least had to reach some rapprochement—with distinctive local modes of dress (see, e.g., Edwards 2001; Barnes and Eicher 1993; Nordholt 1997; Weiner and Schneider 1989). Both the former dominions and colonies, however, have "toyed" with incorporating the "exotic" elements of indigenous dress just as indigenous peoples have appropriated elements of European dress and culture.

The earlier studies of fashion and dress cultures in Australia, Canada, and New Zealand share a concern with demonstrating that each former dominion possessed a stylish culture by tracing the uptake of fashions from Europe, New York, and Hollywood. At the same time, the authors trace the development of local industries of dressmakers, couturiers, fashion and apparel companies and labels, fashion writing and photography, fashion consumption (from mail order to department and specialist stores to boutiques), and the impact of celebrities on fashion and style.

The Canadian study by Routh is a largely conventional costume history that sees dress as encapsulating historical events and social change. While an important source of material concerning the development of Canadian dress codes, Routh emphasizes the derivative nature of Canadian fashion, from both Europe and Canada's neighbor, America. Periodically, elements of Inuit and Indian design have also flavored Canadian approaches to dress, a trend that has become increasingly marked in recent years. She discusses the emergence of distinctive sense of Canadian design and coterie of designers, less in terms of nationalism but rather in terms of the ability of Canadians to compete internationally. Routh (1993: 180) concludes that "Canadians will continue to establish their niche in the fabulous and entertaining, always changing, world of fashion."

Wolfe's study of New Zealand combines a costume history approach with a more wide-ranging discussion. He positions New Zealand dress in relation to other studies of fashion, especially those concerning Australia. While Canada has sought to balance European influences—especially the radically different traditional Scottish and flamboyant French codes—with the encroachment of American fashion imperialism, New Zealand has tussled with influences from Europe, as well as its neighbor and competitor, Australia. For Wolfe, this has been reflected in the development of New Zealand's dress codes over time as well as in specialist production and garments: strong footwear, underwear, and denim industries; traditional school uniforms; bush shirts; black singlets; and jandals. Increasingly, however, New Zealand culture is being shaped by Polynesian and Maori cultures. While Wolfe (2001: 118) cautiously argues that "there may be signs that a style of our own is emerging," he also quotes designer Marilyn Sainty who "believes that New Zealanders may have overtaken the Australians when it comes to stylish dressing" by establishing "a certain definition and difference" (Wolfe 2001: 121).

Taking the earlier studies of "dominion" fashion as a whole, a tone of ambivalence can be detected, veering between what Australians call a "cultural cringe" (slavishly emulating the "center") to jingoistically proclaiming "post-colonial" innovation and uniqueness. The truth undoubtedly lies somewhere in between.

The general contours of fashions, styles, and trends in these post-dominion societies *have* largely emanated from elsewhere but local inflections have become more noticeable and confident over time and in response to particular conditions. For example, in Australia and New Zealand, the centrality of informal clothing reflects the climatic extremes and harsh outdoor life. Specialist garments include the ubiquitous T-shirt, shorts, and thongs in Australia; black singlets and jandals in New Zealand; swimwear, surfwear, and beach wear; and outdoor wear (R. M. Williams' moleskins and boots, Akubra hats in Australia; Swanndri check flannel jackets or bush shirts in New Zealand). Canadians have been preoccupied with appropriate clothing for exceptionally cold weather, giving rise to the popularity of thick woolen Hudson Bay coats, the Red River coat for Quebecois girls (navy blue melton with red flannel lining, red epaulets, red striped seams, and a navy blue Capuchin hood lined with red), Linda Lundstrom's 1980's fashion duffle coats and "LaParkas," and "ethnic" Cowichan sweaters and jackets. Individually and collectively, these earlier studies have provided the building blocks for the more critical analysis offered by Maynard.

While ambivalence can still be detected in Maynard's study, her achievement is to take the analysis of the national element in Australian fashion much further than before. She systematically demonstrates how local concerns came to inflect how Australians clothed themselves and expressed their identity. Themes include leisure; moral conservatism versus exhibitionism; tanning, swimming, and surfing; a preoccupation with Australian fauna, flora, and landscape; and exotic appropriations from aboriginal and migrant cultures. But is this sufficient to declare such diverse apparel as national dress with an intrinsic sense of style?

To begin to answer this question, I would propose that a national sense of fashion or style is the expressive encapsulation of the cultural psyche or *zeitgeist* of a place through its people. This occurs when three realms coalesce: *aesthetics*, *cultural practice* and *cultural articulation*. The *aesthetic* dimension refers to the distinctiveness and recognizability of clothing styles, including motifs (surface expressions of identity), choice of garments, cut and composition, ways of wearing, combinations, and fabrics/materials. *Cultural practice* refers to the uptake and consumption of clothing as either everyday wear or niche wear signaling specific relations with the cultural domain. While local adoption is the central element, this specificity must be recognizable to those from elsewhere who may, in turn, adopt elements of the style to emulate "local-ness" (for example, tourist purchases of akubras, kimonos, sarongs, panama hats, "cowboy boots," Hawaiian hibiscus-patterned shirts, "okanui" shorts, or "ethnic" garments). Accordingly, there must be some continuity of these cultural practices reflected in effective supply, distribution, and believable marketing and representation. The third dimension, *cultural articulation*, refers to the ability of the style or fashion to be projected with confidence to the point where it becomes taken-for-granted or "naturalized" to the point where internal and external perceptions of the essence of national stylistic identity overlap.

While Maynard's analysis offers some evidence towards the formation of an Australian stylistic sensibility, especially in the past three decades, there is still a disjunction between lived clothing cultures (everyday styles) and crafted style (designer fashion) as well as an external perception of Australian dress that has not progressed much beyond "bush" clothes, bikinis and safari suits.

The weight of Maynard's argument rests on her reliance on indigenous motifs as underpinning the emergence of a distinctly Aussie sense of style. In this lively and confident section, Maynard cites the work of designers and collectives such as Jenny Kee, Linda Jackson, Bronwyn Bancroft, Utopia, Tiwi Designs and Balarinji as evidence that indigenous design, pre-European culture, and the centrality of landscape in Australian culture has markedly shaped the Australian way of seeing and expressing itself to create "stylish dressing quite distinct from anywhere else" (p. 181). Maynard distinguishes between the use of indigenous design as an aesthetic inspiration and the appropriation of indigenous design in order to legitimate the popularity of indigenous motifs in Australian design practice. While a long-standing phenomenon, the practice is now more not less controversial.

While she heralds the use of indigenous design influences as the core of Aussie fashion, she underemphasizes the implications of the legitimacy of such appropriations and reworkings, especially when interpreted by non-indigenous designers. Questions of copyright and ownership of images, totems, and land forms are not resolved here. For example, while boomerangs are deemed to be in the general domain of design influences—and therefore fair game for incorporation in design, it is not clear at what point a particular depiction of, say, a kangaroo or "dot painting" treatment of landscape is subject to intellectual property claims.

Indicatively, the use by non-indigenous designer Peter Morrissey of the image of boomerangs in fabric used for dresses and shirts was uncontentious. In contrast, there has been an ongoing simmering debate surrounding his use—and radical manipulation—of the artwork of indigenous painter Jacinta Numina Waugh[2] in recent collections (see Craik 2000). This suggests that the jury is still out both on defining the essence of Australian style and in reconciling its components with the underbelly of Australian cultural history.

Apart from issues of creative ownership, the legitimacy of such examples as encapsulations of Australian cultural identity might also be questioned on the grounds that they are merely the most visually different or striking signs of an antipodean sensibility. In fact, the examples Maynard refers to and her accompanying illustrations are confined to the "high end" of the fashion and style spectrum—from designers who appeal to a well-heeled niche clientele. Moreover, the success of these designers and examples of their work has been relatively short-term and changing.

Insofar as indigenous design has impacted on the general public, it has been through superficial references, particularly through the reproduction of aboriginal designs on T-shirts, ties, scarves, and so on. It might be more indicative of lived Australian style to trace the local inflections found in designers for stores such as Target, Myer, Country Road, Cue, Jeans West, Brothers Nielsen, Billabong or Mambo. The design rationale here may be less "out of line" than "in our own space."

Nonetheless, Maynard succeeds in shifting the focus of debate from the arena of modest social history and chronological cataloging of changing styles to a more dynamic and nuanced appreciation of how an ephemeral cultural form such as clothing is part and parcel of the forging of cultural expression and identity. Whether her study proves that there is "a vibrant subtextual history of Australian style that is unashamedly unique" (p. 181) may be open to question, but her study remains a significant milestone. For nations and societies that are building local identities in the face of global culture, the recognition that fashion and style can effectively project a sense of self is now more pertinent than ever.

Notes

1. I use the term "dominions" deliberately since Australia, Canada, and New Zealand were technically "colonies" for a relatively short time

before they gained self-government. In this sense, they differ from other colonies that were administered by colonial representatives.
2. The agreement of the artist was secured for the original use of her artwork involving a royalty return; however, it is unclear whether that agreement covers manipulation of the image or parts thereof, for example, by different color washes.

References

Barnes, Ruth and Joanne Eicher (eds). 1993. *Dress and Gender: Making and Meaning*. Providence, RI: Berg.

Craik, Jennifer. 2000. "Dress, Body and Identity—Fashioning Australian Bodies and National Culture." Paper presented to the Dress, Body and Identity Conference, Nordiska Museet and the Institute of Folk Life Research, Stockholm, Sweden, 21–22 September.

Edwards, Penny. 2001. "Restyling Colonial Cambodia (1860–1954)." *Fashion Theory* 5(4), pp. 389–416.

Joel, Alexandra. 1998. *Parade. The Story of Fashion in Australia*. Sydney: Harper Collins Publishers.

Martyn, Norma. 1976. *The Look: Australian Women in Their Fashion*. Stanmore, NSW: Cassell Australia Ltd.

Maynard, Margaret. 1994. *Fashioned From Penury. Dress as Cultural Practice in Colonial Australia*. Cambridge, New York and Melbourne: Cambridge University Press.

Nordholt, Henk Schulte (ed.). 1997. *Outward Appearances: Dressing State and Society in Indonesia*. Leiden: KITLV Press.

Routh, Caroline. 1993. *In Style. 100 Years of Canadian Women's Fashion*. Toronto: Stoddart Publishing.

Weiner, Annette and Jane Schneider (eds). 1989. *Cloth and the Human Experience*. Washington, DC: Smithsonian Institute Press.

Wolfe, Richard. 2001. *The Way We Wore. The Clothes New Zealanders Have Loved*. Auckland: Penguin.

Notes for Contributors

Articles should be approximately 25 pages in length and *must* include a three-sentence biography of the author(s). Interviews should not exceed 15 pages and do not require an author biography. Film, exhibition and book reviews are normally 500 to 1,000 words in length. The Publishers will require a disk as well as a hard copy of any contributions (please mark clearly on the disk what word-processing program has been used). Berg accepts most programs with the exception of Clarisworks.

Fashion Theory: The Journal of Dress, Body & Culture will produce one issue a year devoted to a single topic. Persons wishing to organize a topical issue are invited to submit a proposal which contains a hundred-word description of the topic together with a list of potential contributors and paper subjects. Proposals are accepted only after review by the journal editor and in-house editorial staff at Berg Publishers.

Manuscripts
Manuscripts should be submitted to: *Fashion Theory: The Journal of Dress, Body & Culture*. Manuscripts will be acknowledged by the editor and entered into the review process discussed below. Manuscripts without illustrations will not be returned unless the author provides a self-addressed stamped envelope. Submission of a manuscript to the journal will be taken to imply that it is not being considered elsewhere for publication, and that if accepted for publication, it will not be published elsewhere, in the same form, in any language, without the consent of the editor and publisher. It is a condition of acceptance by the editor of a manuscript for publication that the publishers automatically acquire the copyright of the published article throughout the world. *Fashion Theory: The Journal of Dress, Body & Culture* does not pay authors for their manuscripts nor does it provide retyping, drawing, or mounting of illustrations.

Style
U.S. spelling and mechanicals are to be used. Authors are advised to consult *The Chicago Manual of Style (14th Edition)* as a guideline for style. *Webster's Dictionary* is our arbiter of spelling. We encourage the use of major subheadings and, where appropriate, second-level subheadings. Manuscripts submitted for consideration as an article must contain: a title page with the full title of the article, the author(s) name and address, and a three-sentence biography for each author. Do not place the author's name on any other page of the manuscript.

Manuscript Preparation
Manuscripts must be typed double-spaced (including quotations, notes, and references cited), one side only, with at least one-inch margins on standard paper using a typeface no smaller than 12pts. The original manuscript and a copy of the text on disk *(please ensure it is clearly marked with the word-processing program that has been used) must* be submitted, along with black and white *original* photographs (to be returned). Authors should retain a copy for their records. Any necessary artwork *must* be submitted with the manuscript.

Footnotes

Footnotes appear as 'Notes' at the end of articles. Authors are advised to include footnote material in the text whenever possible. Notes are to be numbered consecutively throughout the paper and are to be typed double-spaced at the end of the text. (Do not use any footnoting or end-noting programs which your software may offer as this text becomes irretrievably lost at the typesetting stage.)

References

The list of references should be limited to, and inclusive of, those publications actually cited in the text. References are to be cited in the body of the text in parentheses with author's last name, the year of original publication, and page number—e.g., (Rouch 1958: 45). Titles and publication information appear as 'References' at the end of the article and should be listed alphabetically by author and chronologically for each author. Names of journals and publications should appear in full. Film and video information appears as 'Filmography'. References cited should be typed double-spaced on a separate page. *References not presented in the style required will be returned to the author for revision.*

Tables

All tabular material should be part of a separately numbered series of 'Tables'. Each table must be typed on a separate sheet and identified by a short descriptive title. Footnotes for tables appear at the bottom of the table. Marginal notations on manuscripts should indicate approximately where tables are to appear.

Figures

All illustrative material (drawings, maps, diagrams, and photographs) should be designated 'Figures'. They must be submitted in a form suitable for publication without redrawing. Drawings should be carefully done with black ink on either hard, white, smooth-surfaced board or good quality tracing paper. Ordinarily, computer-generated drawings are not of publishable quality. Color photographs can be accepted but will be reproduced as black and white in the printed version of the journal. Whenever possible, photographs should be 8 x 10 inches. The publishers encourage artwork to be submitted as scanned files (300 dpi or above) on disk or via email. All figures should be clearly numbered on the back and numbered consecutively. All captions should be typed double-spaced on a separate page. Marginal notations on manuscripts should indicate approximately where figures are to appear. While the editors and publishers will use ordinary care in protecting all figures submitted, they cannot assume responsibility for their loss or damage. Authors are discouraged from submitting rare or non-replaceable materials. It is the author's responsibility to secure written copyright clearance on *all* photographs and drawings that are not in the public domain. Copyright should be obtained for worldwide rights and on-line publishing.

Criteria for Evaluation

Fashion Theory: The Journal of Dress, Body & Culture is a refereed journal. Manuscripts will be accepted only after review by both the editors and anonymous reviewers deemed competent to make professional judgments concerning the quality of the manuscript. Upon request, authors will receive reviewers' evaluations.

Reprints for Authors

Twenty-five reprints of authors' articles will be provided to the first named author free of charge. Additional reprints may be purchased upon request.